ONCE UNSPOKEN

A Series of Monologues from the Previously Unheard

MARISSA ALEXA MCCOOL

MEGHANA NALLAJERLA   ANONYMOUS A

AMBER AUSLANDER   AMBER BIESECKER

MELA BLUST   BRAVE CROW   CAREN EVANS

MELINA RAYNA SVANHILD FARLEY-BARRATT

MELISSA FRANK   BETHANY FUTRELL

EMMALIA PETRA FAE GEORGE

SOPHIA GRIFFITH-GORGATI

PRINCESS HARMONY   TANYA JAIN

RENEE JAMES   ANONYMOUS K

DHARMA KELLEHER   JESSICA KIRSCHNER

PEARL LO   ANDREINA LAMAS MATHEUS

AIDEN XAVIER MCCOOL   ANONYMOUS N

KELLIE RAMDEEN   LOGAN REISS

HADAR RUBIN   CONNOR SCARLETT

LAYHA P. SPOONHUNTER   MANDISA THOMAS

CALLIE WRIGHT

Edited by
AMBER BIESECKER

These monologues were compiled with consent and no ownership claimed over their authorship, except the ones written by the main author.

Cover design by Rachael Gunderson

Published by Wyrmwood Publishing & Editing
http://www.wyrmwoodpublishing.com

ISBN-13: 978-1548184551
ISBN-10: 1548184551

This book is dedicated to the memories of

Benedict Frank and Brennan Ebel

FOREWORD

by Meghana Nallajerla

Marissa and I met each other in the basement greenroom of a college auditorium in the spring of 2017. We were both there because we were performers in our college's rendition of *The Vagina Monologues*.

The Vagina Monologues is a show consisting of a series of monologues written in the late 1990s which openly discuss sex, sexuality, and sexual violence. The show is incredibly groundbreaking, bringing to the stage the experiences of survivors of violence in a way that was previously unfathomable.

The show is performed around Valentine's Day every year across the United States and the world. In its almost 30-year run, the show and the community it has created have done much to raise awareness about sexual violence and raise funds supporting organizations that aid survivors.

However, the show was not groundbreaking for everyone. In the same vein as much of cis white, western feminism, the show lacks the narratives of trans women, women of color, and women in post-colonial countries, just to name a few. It has been consistently critiqued for these issues, and many communities have created shows more representative of their own narratives in response.

In backstage conversations between bites of vending-machine snacks, Marissa and I found solidarity in each other. Marissa is the first trans woman to perform in our university's *Vagina Monologues*, which is a show that has historically been transphobic. In my own case, as a woman of color and a South Asian-American woman, the feeling of erasure within both this show and similar feminist spaces on my campus is one that has weighed heavily on me during my own time in college.

When I talked to Marissa about my experiences with white supremacy and racism, she listened patiently and openly. She never spoke over me or tried to defend institutions I critiqued. I have tried to do the same for her, when she has discussed transphobia and cissexism. And I am truly in awe of the result of those conversations—the idea behind this collection.

There have always been incredible black and brown women leading these conversations on my campus and beyond. My experience as one South Asian-American woman, with various marginalized and privileged identities wrapped into one, is not representative of all of us, and it certainly is not representative of all women of color. But that in itself is the point of these stories. They only represent a part of diverse communities, most of whom have been denied a platform historically. To expect one individual from a marginalized racial community to speak for the entire group, however, is one component of white supremacy. It denies us nuance, diversity, and our humanity.

In speaking to my own experience, I hope to share a singular perspective on what it meant for me to live my South Asian brownness. It in no way speaks for anyone other than myself, nor do I intend for it to. Perhaps this experience of marginalization is a truth to other South Asian women and women of color.

It has been, at least, for me.

*Amma** was my first feminist icon. She seemed to navigate the world with confidence and ease, despite moving homes and countries twice over. It seemed like she was strong enough to face the whole world, but at the same time, she loved, soothed, and showed vulnerability.

When I think of my childhood memories of her, I can still see her *kurti* flutter behind her as she weaved through our home managing everything from the mundane to the unthinkable.

Amma was simultaneously critical of white supremacy and patriarchy during my upbringing as a brown girl in the Deep South. When I would come home and cry because white children at school told me I was "so dark," Amma would gently wipe away my tears and hold me while also critiquing racism. When my history teachers taught colonial-apologist narratives of South Asian history, Amma encouraged me to read about the revolutionary freedom fighters and history of resistance in South Asia. If teachers at school asked me inappropriate questions about arranged marriage or how my parents met, Amma could always help me shrug it off.

Just like Amma, her sisters and mother held incredible multitudes within them—they had strength, but showed compassion; they understood resistance, but also care. Ever since I was a child, I admired these women in my family. Without knowing it, I had been raised into an anti-colonial, anti-white supremacist feminism.

My icons, just like myself, are not without their flaws. The feminism I internalized from my family was not critical of caste, Islamophobia, and transphobia, to name only a few. In this sense, it was never fully anti-colonial or critical. I understand now that my privileges allowed me to stay ignorant of these issues, and understanding our privileges and unlearning is a journey we continue to go on together as a family.

While I now challenge much of the feminism I was taught, growing up with the presence of the women in my family nevertheless encouraged me to resist what I found to be wrong, no matter who said it was right.

My family helped me embrace my identity as a South Asian woman in America; I entered feminist spaces on my campus with this background and a heart filled with hope. I expected, both out of naiveté and privilege, to see what I had grown up with reflected in the ideology of my campus feminist peers.

* - *The Telugu word for "Mom."*

❦

I first auditioned for *The Vagina Monologues* as a first-year student at Penn. The director was an incredible artist and woman of color who took me under her wing and helped me become more critical.

But I quickly came to realize that I did not see myself

fully reflected in the mainstream communities and narratives present. I felt I was perceived either as submissive, too aggressive, or faced microaggressions and ignorance from white women in the space.

In my first year in these spaces, I heard individuals lament how oppressed "some women in the East" are, or imply that men of color are more likely to be ignorant of consent.

I felt that the narratives of empowerment and liberation were not inclusive of anti-racist struggle.

Learning about intersectionality and global feminism in my first few years in college, I believed naïvely that I could use this knowledge to help change the demographics and missions of more mainstream feminist spaces on campus. Within the context of *The Vagina Monologues*, I started to wear sarees during my performances. If the show's stories did not reflect me, I hoped at least what I wore partially would.

Every winter when I went home for break, Amma would ask me if I needed something to wear for "that show you're in." We would both sit and dig through her sarees to find something that worked. The first year I performed in the show wearing a saree, I remember making eye contact with a South Asian woman in the audience who smiled at me. It was a momentary acknowledgement, an "I see you." I felt temporarily satisfied.

For the most part, other women in the show seemed encouraging of my decision to wear South Asian clothing. Wearing South Asian clothes in the show quickly became "my thing." People would ask me well-intentioned, but ignorant questions about my nose ring, or touch my saree without my consent. I felt appreciated, but did not know where the line between representation and tokenization laid. It felt as if my nuanced critiques of racism and white-savior feminism were reduced to a costume.

At any rate, this was only a superficial change. What I wore did not change the framework of the show. I constantly felt I was not doing enough to challenge the white, colonial lens of this show, and much of our campus feminist politics.

Mostly, I felt tired. Despite being on campus and in these spaces for over three years, I felt that nothing had changed. I wore my saree every year without fail, answered the same questions, and made the same critique, only to return the next year to say the same thing again.

This is where I was in my journey when I first met Marissa.

At the same time, this is not meant to erase the work of all the black and brown women who were active in feminist spaces on my campus, and in our show, both as performers and board members. Without the community they created, I would not have survived for as long as I did, nor would I have felt encouraged to continue expressing my thoughts and my desire for even more change.

Further, while race has been most salient to my experience, mainstream feminist spaces on campus are plagued by other issues. Transphobia is a major one of them, with little attention being dedicated to trans women's uniquely marginalized experiences—for example the usage of cissexist and isolating rhetoric is still prevalent.

Additionally, I experienced racism as a South Asian woman who is non-black and non-Muslim. Although the term "women of color" is one I find empowering, it in no way captures the diversity and complexities of the communities it describes. Within communities of color, there are hierarchies of power and prejudice, and anti-blackness is a persistent problem across feminist spaces, including ours.

Acknowledging and unlearning anti-blackness, Islamophobia, casteism, classism, and transphobia have been an important part of understanding and contemplating my own privilege. I know that I have undoubtedly not always been the best ally in this journey, and I can only hope to continue to grow through organizing, activism, and *listening*.

If anything, I have learned from my experience that implanting marginalized folks into oppressive structures—such as women of color, trans women, and trans women of color into white, cis spaces—will not modify much unless the *framework* of the space itself is altered. Bringing in and tokenizing marginalized people will do nothing to change a space unless we are actively *centered* in it.

But what does this look like?

It is a difficult question that doesn't have a singular answer. But you may find part of that answer in the pages of this book, though the work neither started nor ends here.

This collection is a gathering for some of us in this show and our campus who have felt un- or underrepresented, but it is not an answer to a systemic problem, nor is it inclusive of everyone who has been denied a platform. To claim that it is would simply be replicating the same oppressive structures we have so vehemently critiqued. These stories are simply *one* avenue for *some* of us. It will undoubtedly take many more such efforts (which many community activists and organizers continue to do every day) to continually critique institutionalized and prevalent cis, straight, white American feminist discourse.

In the meanwhile, I invite other students, performers, activists and those in my own communities—be they feminists on campuses, women of color from different backgrounds, or folks who consider themselves allies—to reflect on this question:

What purpose do spaces like *The Vagina Monologues* serve if they are not truly inclusive of all those they claim to support and represent?

NOT ALL MONOLOGUES ARE UNIVERSAL

ORIGINALLY PUBLISHED IN THE DAILY
PENNSYLVANIAN ON FEBRUARY 19TH, 2018

by Marissa Alexa McCool

My feelings on this show are a series of contradictions.

Not the production or the cast, mind you, but the material itself. It's a vicious circle of wanting to be grateful for someone who has helped the words of feminism and sexual violence awareness reach so many new eyes and ears, but also being aware that the narrative seems directed toward a specific audience, as well as coming from the perspective of one.

Then I feel guilty for not wanting to be the Ungrateful Millennial™, while also acknowledging that at the age of 32, the cast I'm working with grew up in a drastically different world than I did, and their experiences don't relate to this narrative as much. Campus violence, the internet, and social media; three issues ubiquitous to the traditional student attending Penn right now, are glaringly absent from these stories.

I appreciate there being a trans story. Even in 2018, our

visibility is difficult, and to be visible is dangerous. Yet the story itself is problematic, both for story reasons that I don't have the time or space to get into, but also because of how I consider my husband, who is trans in his own right. He was born with a vagina, and the only mention his perspective gets at all is from the board being sure to specify the phrase "women or people born with vaginas."

And while trans women are given that specific monologue, that's the only time they're represented in the entire show. None of the other stories even mention it in passing, as far as I can tell. Not to mention, even as wonderful and sincere as the cisgender performers of the piece are this year, it speaks a bit to the perception the show has that no trans performers are present for that piece. I was cast as a fill-in last year, and somehow in 17 years of the production, that was the first performance to include a trans person.

I appreciate the awareness and attention the show brings to sexual violence. The #MeToo era was possible in part because of the unapologetic assertiveness of this show. Yet the women backstage to whom I speak, who are from marginalized communities, especially POC, struggle to find their voices and representation within these words. Given my aforementioned contradictory feelings of the trans narrative, I can somewhat relate.

I acknowledge how important this show was for women and feminism, and yet for all the good it does, wonder why the license and copyright are so stringent, to the point that I wrote my own monologue speaking to my experience last year and couldn't perform it because of the difficulties with the license that prevent performers from bringing their personal experiences to this show, which is supposed to speak of personal experience.

Performing my own piece this year comes with the

acknowledgement that I am a spotlight performer coming in from the outside world as a Penn alum, and that's a huge deal, considering it was out of the question last year. If the point of the show is to speak for women, why make it so difficult for women to speak their own words?

However, the place I harbor no contradictions is my love for the production of the show and its cast.

Last year, not a single member of the cast questioned my gender or my being there (that I heard of). Before the show, in an intimate gathering where everyone was free to speak, I read the monologue I wrote and felt nothing but welcomed, protected, and loved. This year was more of the same.

I was blown away by the disclaimers these brave people put into the opening of the show, acknowledging these same tangled webs that I've mentioned and beyond. I imagine that, like me, it's the community of the production and the truly safe place within it that draws so many back, despite the problematic nature of the show itself.

In the first interaction I had with a cast member in the locker room, they mentioned how cisnormative the show is. Some spoke of their trans friends who refuse to attend this show for that reason, and I can't blame them. The awareness and empathy I've observed and experienced from this production are second to none. That's why driving the entire way from Saint Paul was worth it.

As I write this story from my hotel room after the Friday night show, I can't help but share what I told my husband once we were in the car. After he had dried my tears of gratitude from the countless cast members and people from the audience saying such wonderful things to me and giving me hugs (all of whom asked first, which was amazing in and of itself), I spoke of the age and generation difference between myself at age 32 and the cast and production team, who were 10-14 years younger. I said if these are the people who are going to run the world, we're going to be okay. We're going to make it.

It was this show, even with its well-documented problems, that made that experience possible. I can also say that the community and the safety felt within it are what have brought people like me back, and I know I don't only speak for myself in that regard.

Written on Friday night between productions of 2018's V-Day

PROLOGUE

by Marissa Alexa McCool

NOT EVERYTHING IS THE SAME.

Not everyone has the same experience, and it's time we stop pretending they do.

Some can sit comfortably during a show called *The Vagina Monologues* and not think twice about whose voices aren't included.

Some cannot.

This is a story for them.

When I heard that trans people weren't willing to come to the show, I had to stop myself from asking why.

Reflecting on my experience trying to perform my
    own words,
Not being cast in the trans piece,
Being the only trans person there,
Cis people performing the trans monologue
That in and of itself tied our identity to the vagina.
On one hand, sure, it's to be expected.
It's in the name of the show.
But when I get my science vagina installed later
    this year,
It won't be what makes me a woman.
Getting my name changed
Wasn't what made me a woman.
Getting my birth certificate corrected
Wasn't what made me a woman.
I am who I say I am,
And you do not have more of a right to that
Than I do.

Trans men are invisible in that show.
Non-binary people are invisible in that show.
The one trans woman experience they share
Is of a straight trans woman,
And it ends in murder and tragedy.
There are so many amazing trans stories to be told.
Some of them you will hopefully find here.

I heard Meghana express how she truly felt,
How she never felt welcome in these circles,
An outsider to this community.
I saw the women of color nodding in agreement,
And I noticed once again.

I was the only trans woman in the room.
It wasn't but a few minutes later
Before someone chimed in
About how her mom liked 90s feminism
And that made it okay.
We've got a long way to go.

I've tried to gather as many voices as I could.
Some I've known for years.
Some I'm in love with.
Some I live with.
Some I met at Penn in that show.
Some I've interviewed on the shows.
Some I've never met.
Some I may never meet.
All of their voices are valid and needed to be heard,
Their stories told,
Their lives shared,
Even if they couldn't do it without anonymity.

These are their monologues,
Essays,
Poems,
Rants,
Expressions,
Tragedies,
Triumphs,
Survivals,
Trials,
And moments of epiphany.
I hope you get as much out of their stories
As I had the privilege to learn

Through meeting and conversing
With all who participated.
Those who were unspoken...
Once.

❦ I ❦

A YEAR AS MYSELF

(2018)

by Marissa Alexa McCool

When I was sixteen years old,
A guy named Will said
That I would one day
Be working for him.
Going to community college
Was going to land me a job
With someone like him
Signing my paychecks.

When I was twenty-eight years old,
A girl named Amanda,
Convinced I was a fetish,
Someone to be used
For her own entertainment
And pleasure,
Put her hand around my throat

After I'd said "no!"
After I'd resisted
After I said I didn't want it,
And she choked me
Until I stopped resisting.

It seems like a different lifetime
When those words were spoken
To a false representation
Of a person
I pretended to be,
For that person's name
Is not the one inscribed
On my Penn diploma.
I didn't go to graduation
Because the previous year,
A certain man was in attendance
About whom I'd written a book
That started with the words
"Fuck you."

I did attend LGBT graduation,
Where I listened to a speech
That lauded Penn's inclusivity
And protections
That included gender identity.

I was followed into a bathroom
Despite having a friend with me,
Despite having that friend vouch for me,
And I was questioned
Humiliated
Embarrassed

Ashamed.
My friend's word wasn't enough
My word wasn't enough
My name wasn't enough
My ID wasn't enough
Because someone supposedly
Saw a guy go in there
And Marissa
She said
Could be a gender-neutral name
Apparently

Three months earlier,
I'd stood on this very stage
Performing under my true name
My true identity
My true self
With my words published in the program
Proclaiming who I am loudly
Proudly
Assertively

I AM MARISSA.

In this place, on this stage,
While shooting video for the team,
Backstage before each show,
On Locust Walk
On my diploma
In the articles in the *Daily Pennsylvanian*
On my book
My podcasts
On Canvas

On my Penn ID
But after all that, there I stood
Because a security guard
In the cafeteria
Didn't believe my friend
Who said I was
Who I was
Didn't believe me
When I said
Who I was
And didn't believe that name
That was emblazoned
On book covers and
Podcast guest lists.

At that moment,
I was only a suspicion.

If that's what it's like
For someone known and protected
By the institution itself
What must it be like
For the trans girl
Who doesn't have the platform
The friends in the theater
Or the access to a voice
Or the safety to scream
In the hate pastor's face?
She's the one I think of most
The one who's gone with me this past year

Had that adamant "fuck you"
Come from someone aged 18

Instead of 31...
It cannot be understated
The regret
that seeps in
Upon knowing
who you truly are
And wondering
how life
Could've been

Those 13 years
Spent barely visible in the closet
Could've been spent
Protecting someone
Who didn't have a closet
To hide in.

I spent that year
Traveling the country
Speaking words
But hearing more
In Hickory, North Carolina,
A father confessed to me
The difficulty he'd gone through
In learning what trans meant
Because his daughter was trans,
And words I'd spoken
Had helped him learn
How to love who his daughter was
Instead of who he thought she was.

I performed a cold open
In Allentown, PA

Fast-delivering a poem I'd written
And deciding to use that
Instead of an introduction.
My words reached people
In a way
They never could've
Before I was me
Because the real me
Was the one who had been asked
To give them.

I received a standing ovation
In Carlisle, PA, where I grew up
For the piece I'd written
Partially published in this program
At their show last year
When the director threw out the script.
The only people who had heard it
Prior to that day
Were the ones who joined
In a private circle
Before this show last year,
The first show in the 17 years
Of Penn V-Day
To include trans people.

I walked in Salt Lake City
As no less than 20 people
Shouted slurs as they drove or passed by.
I spoke to Flint natives
And indigenous folk
From Standing Rock
On a summer day in Michigan

Wondering why I was the one speaking
When they had stories to tell.

I stood in the botanical gardens
In Gainesville, Florida
As a trans girl also dealing with chemo
Hugged me for five minutes
After I told her
I'd helped her complete
The fundraising she needed
For bottom surgery.

A trans girl in Scotland
Who told me
That my weekly show of trans jokes
Helped her get through
The roughest year of her life.

The professor
Who took me to dinner
To learn more about our community,
To be a better ally.

My internet son
Who can't be himself
Because his birth parents
Have put the condition on him
That love comes with a price.

The abuse survivor
Who told her story
On my show
To help others

Avoid the same situation.

A non-binary person
Meeting me in Seattle at a show
For other podcasters
I'd once thought out of my league
But had since befriended me.
They fell in love with me
And moved to Saint Paul
To keep an eye on me
When my husband needed a break
From dealing with my
Overwhelming wifely ass.

My girlfriend
The raven-haired songbird
Who tells me I'm beautiful
Even when I don't feel like it.
And who will also
Protest her value
At deserving to be in this.

And of course,
The man who made me his wife
Because he fell in love with the person
And the gender didn't matter.

When I wrote my piece
A year ago, for this show,
It was filled with my history
And all the vitriol I'd built up
In finally declaring to the world
Who I really was.

This year,
I face the fear of the unknown
As the date
For the installation
Of my shiny new science vagina
Finally approaches.
Wondering what feeling correct
In entirety, my body matching my spirit
Will bring to my life
When everything else
Has matched up so well?

But, I also feel guilt
Which transfers into rage
Because for all the luck
I've received in my transition
And journey,
For the platforms I've been given
The space in people's headphones
The words on hundreds of pages

Why did it take
Screaming in a hate pastor's face,
Going to a school that defends our right to exist,
Podcasting for our community,
and speaking out at a convention
For me to be treated
The exact same way
That every trans person who comes out
Should be?

I may be able to write

But I'm not special
When it comes to my name
And identity.
Every name I read
Every year
On the Trans Day of Remembrance
Is one more name
That didn't have to be there.
Whether it's because comedians
Still defend using us as punchlines,
Because ignorant people think they know better,
Because well-intentioned people want an ally
    cookie,
Or because people think we deserve to die
For existing.

I should not be treated better
Just because
I'm the first trans person
That you ever met in person
And therefore could put a face on the issue.
How about treating us fairly
Because we're fucking people
And not because of all the work I've done
Meaning I've somehow "earned it" in your eyes?

When trans people tell you who they are,
Believe them.
When someone tells you their pronouns,
Believe them.
When someone tells you their name,
Believe them.
Even if you're against the singular they.

We don't have to get surgery
To be who we are.
We don't have to go on hormones
To be who are are.
We don't have to "pass" by your standards
To be who we are.

I speak now
Because so many can't.
And in November,
We'll have to read another list of names
Because others will never have the chance to.
Help us reduce the list.
Help us. Respect us. Believe us.
All of us,
Not just me,
Because I wouldn't have the chance
To speak here
Without many others
Fighting and dying in the process
For our right to not be murdered,
Raped,
Discriminated against,
Exiled,
Hated,
Told we're mentally ill,
Deadnamed,
Misgendered,
Harassed,
Assaulted,
Beaten up,
Bullied,

Mocked,
Punchlined,
Or otherwise harmed
For no other reason
than existing.

Help us reduce that list.
Help us keep them safe.
Don't wait until we're standing there
To defend us to your friends.
Correct them. Stand up for us.
WE ARE HERE.
WE EXIST.
WE ARE VALID.

🌿 2 🌿

OVERCOMING SHAME

by Callie Wright

IT WAS SUMMER 2010. MY BAND WAS ON TOUR. WE were living the dream.

Well, kinda.

Touring is a lot less glamorous when you're an unsigned band playing at hole in the wall bars, sleeping on living room floors, and eating ramen every day.

But none of that mattered. This was all I wanted in life.

As we were making an overnight drive between Texas and Louisiana—at the time, ostensibly seven dudes together in a van—I'm guessing it's no surprise that sex was a topic of conversation, yeah?

Someone had the brilliant idea to initiate a group discussion by asking the question: "What's the most out there thing you've ever done sexually?"

My first thought was *Holy shit, I have to answer this question last.* At the time, I was pretty well convinced I was the only kinky person in the world. So I figured the smart thing to do was to listen to everyone else's answers and just sort of give an answer that was in line with what everyone else was saying. I didn't think they would gonna get the whole "this one time, I was mummified in duct tape" thing.

Then something amazing happened. As we went around the circle, I heard more and more stories about all the kinky stuff my friends were into. Well, except for one of us. There's always that one. "I just like having sex, I don't know what the fuck is wrong with you guys." Fucking bass players, man...

These guys were my best friends in the world. It's not like this was the first time sex had ever come up as a topic. How did I not know this?

Just as importantly... why was I so scared for them to find out those things about me?

I was ashamed. Shame is a powerful thing. It controls us, silences us, beats us up inside. It takes so much of the joy out of so many things we do.

I'm a person who has a lot to be ashamed of, if my cultural programming is to be believed. I'm atheist, I'm trans, I'm queer, I'm a woman, I used to be fat, I've lost a bunch of weight and now have a whole bunch of extra skin that's supposed to be ugly and shameful, I have a face and a voice that have stereotypically masculine features, despite my not being a man.

In a lot of ways, my cultural programming has told me that I should absolutely fucking *hate* myself. And you know what? Sometimes I do.

In some form or another, this is pretty near universal, right? For instance, in a survey conducted by Yahoo! Health, they found that 94% of teen girls have been body shamed in their lives. 64% of teen boys have been body shamed too. I couldn't find any survey or specifics for non-binary folks (sorry, I tried, non-binary friends). But that's just one example of one specific kind of shame, and it's *that* prevalent.

Friends, what the fuck are we doing to ourselves?

And I think, to some extent, we know the answer to this, right? That kind of shame is created by people who want us to feel bad about ourselves so they can sell us the shit we need to feel better.

"You know what? You're super ugly, you're fat, you have hair in places we've decided you shouldn't have it, but for the low, low price of $19.95 (plus shipping and handling), we can grant you permission to feel good about yourself again with this new, amazing product from Brand X. Order now. Supplies are limited.

"You're a terrible person who does terrible things because some bitch ate an apple in a garden a few thousand years ago. So honestly, you're kind of the source of everything wrong with the world. But you can be redeemed by showing the proper fealty to the Lord. All it takes is an acknowledgment of just what a piece of shit you are, how dependent you are on us to get better, and 10% of your income every Sunday. You know... for the lord."

Cultural programming is powerful. Daniel Quinn, one of my favorite authors, calls this entity "Mother Culture." Mother Culture whispers in our ear all the things we're supposed to believe, even before we're born. The world even expects us to experience life in a certain way based on the genitals doctors see in the sonogram. We have these nice, neat and tidy blue or pink boxes being built for us before we even enter the world.

And it's important to point out that this is a thing we're all subject to. I don't say all this to imply that if you feel pressured to fit these norms or take action to fit them, that you're somehow weak or lesser than. I also don't mean to say that if these cultural norms happen to fit your actual tastes or your identity, that you should be ashamed of that. It's okay to be who you are.

This is just to say that this pressure is powerful. It's suffocating for those of us it doesn't fit. We all feel it, and we all adapt to it in different ways. And I think it's an important thing to be aware of.

So I want to tell you a few stories about overcoming some of those feelings, some stories of *not* overcoming those feelings, and maybe, hopefully, there'll be something in there for you to take away.

Shame is actually one of the first emotions I remember feeling in even a superficial realization of my identity. I remember literally thinking, *I was supposed to be a girl!* and my next thought was, *Whoa, what's wrong with me?* Even as a kid, I knew intuitively that it was bad for boys to have feminine interests or characteristics. I dwelled on this so much that it became an obsession.

I knew at least on some level who I was, I knew the stigma attached to that, and so the taboo turned into an obsession. I had myself convinced for a long time that my identity was actually a fetish.

I'm not sure how many of you are familiar with the fetish world, but there's a category of fetish play called sissi-fication or forced feminization. The focus of this is more or less the humiliation that comes with being a man and being forced into a feminine presentation or feminine role.

Now, I'm not a big fan of saying what I think is going on in other people's heads, so I'm not making a pronouncement about the entirety of this phenomenon, but I'll tell you what I think was going on in my own head.

I craved emasculation because masculinity didn't fit me. It wasn't who I was. I desperately needed the relief that came from letting go of the masculine role that'd been assigned to me at birth. It became such an overriding obsession that it was an unbelievable thrill to shed that masculinity.

Doing it in the context of the fetish world made it easier too. I could hide the real reason I was into it. It was easier for me to say I got off on the humiliation than to just say "this is who I actually am."

As I was able to indulge in this more and more with a partner I had at the time, the shame started to fall away. I'd met someone who didn't see anything wrong with these needs. She helped me feel normal about my femininity. I started to realize there was more going on than just a fetish.

I finally worked up the courage to Google the term "transgender," and my life changed forever.

And when I did finally come out, I knew so little about gender. I was that insufferable douche that got all "well, actually" when people would start to talk about misogyny or racism, or pretty much any other -ism that deals with dynamics of privilege and oppression. I still had *a lot* to learn and unlearn. And one of my first lessons actually happened at the grocery store.

It was the first time I went grocery shopping after I'd started to present in a more femme way. I had this sweet, green striped dress from Torrid, a super cute cardigan from Lane Bryant, a purse from Target, and some shoes my ex gave me. I nervously walked into Kroger's shaving aisle, and it was there I received one of my first lessons about the way society treats you differently based on your gender, and some of the unique ways this affects trans people.

Now that I'd realized and accepted the fact that I was a

woman, the only proper thing for me to do was to shop in the women's section of the shaving aisle, right? It was time for the pink and purple razors and the shaving creams that moisturized and had pictures of flowers on the can. That was what I was supposed to want, right? And I do like pink and purple. And I like flowers.

What I'm not a fan of is paying more for those things.

Raise your hand if you've heard of the pink tax. It's the name for the phenomenon where products marketed toward women cost more than products marketed toward men, even if they serve the same function. On average, personal care products marketed toward women cost about 13% more than products marketed toward men.

So the practical side of me said, *Razors are razors and shaving cream is shaving cream. You're not doing so hot financially. Get the cheaper shit that does the same job, because that's the sensible thing to do!*

As I walked over to the men's aisle, intent on getting the stuff I'd always used instead, I had a thought.

I was not at all confident in my appearance, my voice, or my presentation. I was already sure that everyone in the world was staring at me and mocking me for being trans. My confidence in my identity was shaky, at best. If I went and shopped in the men's aisle, wouldn't I be admitting that a man was who I actually was?

No, that's silly. It's a fucking razor and shaving cream. This is ridiculous.

But wait... I'm presenting femme, buying men's stuff, and I have too many groceries to use the self-checkout, so I have to deal with a cashier. And they'll see the blue and green designs on the shaving cream cans and the very un-pink and un-purple razors, and they're gonna start asking questions. If someone clocks me, I could be in real danger from a safety standpoint.

I was already worried someone was going to figure me out and beat me up. I didn't want to make it even more obvious.

And this was when it started to hit me. Is this really the world we've created with gendered products and gendered expectations and the culture of shame that comes with stepping outside of those norms and expectations?

Sadly, the answer is yup, it sure is! And I went ahead and paid the extra 13% for my pink and purple razor and my moisturizing shaving cream with the flowers on the can.

I gave in, partially for safety reasons, partially because I was convinced that's what I was supposed to do if people were really to accept me as a woman.

It's interesting how different my experience is now, five years or so later. It's not that those feelings and pressures are gone, but I definitely feel less compelled to alter myself to fit them.

When I came out, I don't think I wore pants for like, two years—skirts and dresses only. *Women things.* Without noticing it, though, I eventually started to drift the other direction in my presentation. I subconsciously started to collect flannel and skinny jeans.

I went shoe shopping a few months ago. I looked through the women's section, didn't see anything I liked, and I just sort of casually strolled over to the men's section to see if there was anything I liked there. It took about 10 minutes for it to dawn on me that a few months ago, I would've been terrified to do this.

So I just smiled and I bought the men's shoes I'm wearing on this stage right now. Not even a single fuck given.

So what made the difference for me? I can point to a few things.

A big one is probably the fact that I had my bottom surgery eight months ago. I'm comfortable enough in my own body that I'm thinking less about the ways I'm different, and I think on my gender identity less than I used to. It makes me more able to just do the shit I want to do.

I also have to look at the power of my community's affirmation of me. I feel less like I need to constantly signal to the world who I am. My family, my friends, and my community, including you in this room, have embraced me with open arms and shown me on no uncertain terms that you do recognize me for who I am. That removes pressure.

And I think I eventually just hit a tipping point where that pressure and the shame that comes from not living up to gendered expectations became background noise.

It's still there. I still feel it sometimes. Sometimes it gets me down still. But it's certainly not a primary concern in my life anymore, and so I'm able to indulge in the stuff that's really me instead of worrying about how it might look to others.

Notice I didn't say that I built myself up into a badass, threw my middle finger up at society, and said "Fuck you all, I'm gonna do me!" It takes a community to raise a baby transling. This isn't something most of us can do on our own.

Human beings are often most comfortable in binary worlds. We like simple answers. We like to know what's going on, who's safe and who's not, who's in our circle and who's outside of it. When we're reminded that things just aren't that simple, it often makes us super uncomfortable.

Using gender as an example, I'm gonna go out on a limb here and say that I think maybe on some level, almost everyone realizes just how fragile this construct is as our society prescribes it. It's so fragile a construct, in fact, that it apparently crumbles under the weight of someone with a penis wearing a dress. On one level or another, we recognize this fragility and are threatened by the existence of people who challenge that safe, comfortable, simple binary.

But often, we try really hard to believe what we're taught, because it gives us answers. It gives us a system to organize the world by, and that's comfortable. Trans people are a threat to that comfort. And I think that explains at least some of the world's hostility to us. I think it also explains some of why so many trans folks have trouble accepting ourselves.

So this brings me to where I am today. Frankly, I'm sick the fuck to death of being told what I should and shouldn't be ashamed of by shitty people.

If you're sitting in this room, as an atheist, as a queer person, as a trans person, as a woman, as anything other than society's default, you know these feelings on some level, I have no doubt. You've been told that who you are, the core of your being, what you know about the world, and what you know about yourself is something to be ashamed of. At best, it's something to hide or downplay; at worst, it's something to hate yourself for.

You might've been told that you're responsible for the fall of man, for natural disasters, for tragedies that happen in your communities, or that you are the source of the utter moral decadence so evident in our society today.

I'm here to tell you, friends, that if you're that threatening to shitty people, then I think you're a goddamned superhero. You're a fucking force of nature. You really and truly do have power. Why else would these people be so terrified of you? You're too real for them. You're too good.

And it's okay if it doesn't always feel that way, truly it is. Life doesn't work like some silly motivational speech where if you just repeat some positivity mantra all day, all your problems disappear. That's bullshit. Let's talk about what's real, though.

What's real is that the voice of Mother Culture that tells you that who you are is wrong is a fucking *liar*.

What's real is that if you're lost, you're hurting, you're scared, or if you feel like no one cares and no one understands, you need to know that that there's a community out here who loves you, cares for you, and knows that you're capable of amazing things, and that you are *worthy* of love.

And so when I feel like it, I'm going to lie in bed and cry about how awful people make me feel. Because it's okay to do that. But when I can, I'm going to stand up. I'm gonna put my middle fingers in the air, let my bat wings fly, scream in my masculine-sounding voice with my lesbian ass flannels and skinny jeans, with my foul-ass, unladylike language:

"This is *me,* motherfuckers. Expect me, expect my community. You can get on board, or you can get steamrolled, because we're coming either way!"

3

SEXY SECULAR WOMAN

by Mandisa Thomas

IN THE SUMMER OF 2012, I WAS ASKED TO PARTICIPATE in a calendar project that was being put on by the newly formed organization, Secular Woman. It was a fundraising effort that was to feature some prominent atheists from diverse backgrounds and body types.

The concept? Nude to partially nude photos that celebrated sexuality and body positivity.

I was very excited and jumped at the chance. Nudity, positive body expression and sexual liberation are near and dear to me—particularly for women who don't fit the typical beauty standards. I am a black woman who is a size 18. Nowhere do I fit in to those standards—nor did I ever care to. I guess that was part of it—getting to unwrap more of my unconventional side.

It was also an honor to be considered prominent,

because I was still new to the community at that time. I had founded my organization, Black Nonbelievers, in 2011, and had become heavily involved in the atheist/secular community, but was still relatively unknown.

I discussed this with my husband. While I was all set and ready to take fully nude photos, I had to consider my job, his thoughts, and our family.

Well, he was dead-set against full nudity—something I challenged him on, considering all the photos of nude women that he had saved on our computer.

He said, "Well, they aren't my wife!"

I responded, "Should that make a difference?! I don't have a problem with you looking at those women. In fact, I like looking at them too! Also, we are not each other's *property*, and we don't subscribe to 'traditional' marriage values anyway—we think they're bullshit!"

We eventually discussed this some more, and agreed that I would do partially nude, but mostly suggestive photos for the project.

The day of the shoot was the first time in a while that I had makeup applied. I was never much for it—my mother, while not religious, was conservative when it came to beauty enhancements. I only wore it during performances when I was younger, and rarely even then.

Prior to this shoot, I had taken photos for the billboard campaign for African Americans for Humanism. Those came out nice, but of course, it was a different premise altogether.

My photographer, a former coworker and good friend, and I discussed the theme: sexy and seductive. I was to make the most appropriate faces and gestures for this theme, and boy, did I.

The backdrop was the fireplace in the den area of my home. My hair was laid, my makeup was on point, and I felt *fly* (I know I'm dating myself with that term).

I was still nervous—after all, I was about to bare more than usual, and in anticipation of a broad audience. And this was still the first professional shoot of its kind for me. As much as I had admired such work from afar, I was going to become part of it—which was kind of scary.

But my passion and convictions about body expression overcame that fear. I had to practice what I preached.

During the shoot, I imagined that I was an exotic dancer —enticing with my body and my mind. I simulated masturbation, imagining my sexual fantasies coming true. Some of my favorite music came to mind as well—*Erotic City* by Prince, *Juicy Fruit* by Mtume, and *Take You Down to Love* by Patrice Rushen.

In less than two hours, there were over 100 photos taken. My photographer said I made his work easy.

When the photos were delivered to me, I was in awe of what was captured. All my life, my looks were remarked by others, but as I mentioned before, my mother was conservative and emphasized in her own way a focus on education.

She did this by downplaying my looks, and even yelled at me one time because I came home with lipstick on in high school. A friend had suggested I put some on, and I received many compliments. But I made the mistake of wearing it home, where I was berated and humiliated. So I never did that again.

The photos made me more aware of my beauty and sex appeal. It also helped to understand that there was nothing wrong with accentuating physical appearance, especially for one's self. That it didn't have to be done for the validation of others. Most importantly, it fell in line with my activism and my stance on women's empowerment, that sex appeal can incorporate beauty *and* brains at the same time, especially for this black atheist woman who was a size 18.

As I was submitting the photos that were chosen for the calendar, I was informed that the project had unfortunately been canceled. This was, of course, disappointing, but then I thought, *Why not share them on my Facebook page?* It made no sense for them to go to waste.

I had pondered a similar project for my organization, Black Nonbelievers. But I could always go back and take more photos for that.

Even in my fervor, I felt nervous too. I mean, what if they were reported as indecent? And what about negative and hurtful comments, and all the people who would say "I expect better from *you,* Mandisa"—something I've heard all my life.

But I said fuck it, and posted the ones best suited.

The feedback was overwhelmingly positive. Yes, there were some direct and indirect negative comments, but most of the remarks were how beautiful and sexy the photos were. I was even told by one individual that his bisexual woman friend masturbated to them. Yes, that was *very* flattering!

Much of the feedback was from *other women,* some who said they were encouraged by my bravery. Ironically, I didn't see it as being brave; I was simply being *me.* But in the process of being myself, I learned that I was inspiring others, and more importantly, inspiring myself.

For the first time, I saw what others saw in me—a beautiful, confident, assertive, smart and sexy secular woman. There are plenty of us in the world, and we're still navigating and redefining the societal and narratives of what we are *supposed* to be. We don't do so in the same way, and I don't think we should.

But if we're enriching those around us *and* ourselves, then we're on the right side of this fight.

4

ODE TO THE BLOCKED

by Marissa Alexa McCool

You ain't a girl, you a man
You aren't a pretty girl
You're fucking ugly
Jesus, keep it to yourself
Why would you ever talk about this?
Why would you ever want to do this?
Are you sure you don't have multiple personality
     disorder?
Are you sure you're not just depressed?
Are you sure you're not just confused?
Are you sure you're not just a drag queen?
Are you sure you're really Marissa?

Why can't you just be gay?
Why can't I use the pronouns I know you by?
Why can't I call you the name you were born with?

Why aren't you just that name?
Why aren't you just that body?
Why wouldn't you want to keep it?
Why wouldn't you want to have more kids?
What will the kids say?
What will the parents say?
What will other people's parents say?
What will other people say?
How will you ever get a girlfriend acting like this?
Don't you want to be a provider?
Don't you want to step up and be a man?
Don't you want to be a man?
Aren't you a man?

You're just you to me
You've always just been you
Your gender doesn't matter to me
Your genitals don't matter to me
Nobody cares about your genitals
Gross, do you still have a dick?
Are you going to get surgery?
Are those tits real?
You're so tall
How will you ever pass?
Why can't you just do it in private?
Why should we have to change?
Why should we have to be different?
We don't have to accept you

I'm not transphobic, but
I just don't want a dick
I just don't consider you a real woman
I'm straight, sorry

You're really cute and everything
But I just like vaginas
You understand, right?
I'm straight
Not gay
That's all that matters
It would be a deal-breaker
It's confusing
How would I explain to my parents
That I'm dating a tranny?

Faggot
Queen
Pillow-biter
Queer
Tranny
She-male
Lady-boy
Dude in a dress
Fake woman
Not a woman
It's just science
It's just biology
It's just Jesus
It's just reality
It's just my opinion, man

You need to calm down
You need to understand other opinions
You're immature
You're lazy
You're pretentious
You're dramatic

You need to lay off the sensitivity hormones
Were you always this much of a bitch?
You're just too much for me
You need to stop being so defensive
Not everyone is staring at you
Not everyone is afraid of you
Not everyone wants to hurt you

How will you ever get a girlfriend acting like that?
Stop saying no and shut up
Just let me touch you
Fine, stop being such a bitch
Stop resisting
Stop it
Stop it
Take it, bitch
Take it
This is what happens when you play hard to get
This is what happens when you dress the way
    you do
This is what happens when you are who you are
This is what happens
When you're transgender

You deserve it
You asked for it
You should expect it
What do you expect, look where you are
If you've got a penis, use the men's room
If you're a trans in the men's room, I'll kick your ass
If my masculinity is so fragile, let me hit you
There's no sexism anymore
Feminism isn't necessary

Feminism is outdated
Feminists hate men
Feminists don't need to include trans women
All women have vaginas
All women were born women
This is how you really feel
This is how you need to act
This is how you need to feel
This is how you need to change
This is how you need to be
To make it easier on me

You give a bad name to trans women
You're too radical
You're too angry
You're too bold
You're too confrontational
Nothing's ever going to change their mind
Why even bother?
Why not just stealth it?
Can't you hide your breasts?
Who cares what they think?
Just ignore it, they'll go away
Just use the family bathroom
What do you expect, it's their opinion
It's how they were raised
It's how they were taught
It's how they were shown religion
It's not something they can identify with

If you cut it off, won't it hurt?
If you get the surgery, you'll still be a man
You'll still be a man

You'll always be a man
You can't change gender
Gender and sex are the same
Gender and sex can't be changed
I have more of a right to your identity than you do
I know better than you
You're just confused
You're just lost
You're just brainwashed
You're just young and stupid
You're being manipulated by your professors
You're on drugs
You're going to hell
You have no respect for your spouse
How do you think they feel?
How do you think I feel?
It's going to take time to adjust
Didn't you think about how this would affect me?
Are you sure this is right?
Are you sure this is you?
Are you sure?

Hate.

5

MARISSA

by Pearl Lo

I MET MARISSA IN MY FIRST SEMESTER AS A FRESHMAN at Penn. We were in the same Introduction to Acting class and I was an eager, naïve freshman ready to make my mark at Penn. Little did I know that this class would introduce me to one of the most inspirational people I've ever met.

Our class was very small, but this allowed for an intimate setting people could express themselves in without fear of judgment. I remember being in awe at how everyone, especially Marissa, was so open to committed to their roles. She was always fearless.

I didn't know Marissa as Marissa yet, but I could always tell she was special. She emanated a passion and genuine aura that is rare to come by. I didn't know too much about her life, but I could tell she was an incredibly complex and dedicated person.

She explained to me how she commuted for hours each day to get to Penn. She's a caring parent, and she still managed to take rigorous classes at an Ivy League institution. I honestly have no idea how she was able to manage it all. But she did, because she's one of the strongest people I know.

It's hard to put into words the impact that Marissa had on me from the very beginning, but I hope that this anecdote might provide a small glimpse into how compassionate she is.

As a freshman, it's hard to figure out what you're supposed to be doing. I knew I liked to perform, but it was Marissa who made me feel validated in what I was doing. I had just performed a monologue, and I felt a little uncertain about it. I knew I was being judged and critiqued by my professor. But Marissa told me she was writing a play, and that if it was selected for a competition, she would love to have me act in it.

At that moment, my heart was filled with such joy to know that someone valued me and what I offered as a person. Marissa has that ability to produce that joy in each person she encounters. That moment was one of the defining events that compelled me to pursue the performing arts during my time at Penn.

Throughout the next couple years, I had some smaller interactions with Marissa. We were in the same Cinema Studies class and she always sat in front of me. She was tall, and sometimes I had a hard time seeing over her head, but really, I didn't even mind because it was her. She provided wonderful insights into the class and I appreciated all she had to offer to class discussions.

I wish I had taken this opportunity to get to know

Marissa better, but I'm grateful that eventually came at a later time. However, I was fortunate enough to see some of the wonderful, defining moments in her life. She was so happy when she got married to her wonderful husband, Aiden, and I am so glad to see how happy they are together now.

Our Cinema Studies class came and went, and in the blink of an eye, I was a senior. In my final year at Penn, I wanted to make a difference in the organization that made such an impact on my undergraduate career. And so I became the director the Penn's V-Day moment and the show it produces, *The Vagina Monologues*.

The show and movement have been healing experiences for me that have provided me with an amazing, supportive community and sense of strength. But being the director was not always easy. I was critical of the show and its focus on the vagina being representative of womanhood. I was not a fan of its lack of diversity in the multiple of populations it should be representing. And also, it was very outdated and not modified to fit into the cultural issues that are affecting us today.

In addition to these issues, I found that people were dropping out of the show for multiple reasons. I found that there were several spots I needed to fill. And I knew that I couldn't just fill them with anyone.

For me, the show is not a show. It is not a performance. You should not be casting the most talented actress if they do not stand for what the movement is about. Despite the problematic elements of the show, these are still real women's experiences, and they need to be respected as such.

I wanted to honor these brave women who bared their

souls by casting femme-identifying individuals who would inspire others by representing people who looked like them up on stage. They needed to care about and believe in the movement to end gender-based violence. That was and still is very important to me.

This takes me back to the position I was in where I need to cast people to fill certain roles. I was at lost for who I should reach out to. I knew immediately that I would love for Marissa to be involved, but I didn't know how to approach her about it.

I was nervous because I admired her and respected her so much. I was able to watch her grow and transition into the woman she is today, and I most certainly did not want to make her feel like I was showcasing her simply because of her identity.

But wow, was I impressed by her activism and her strength. I needed her to be a part of my show, and so I finally mustered up the strength to ask if she would be interested.

She was so warm and receptive that I couldn't believe that I had been hesitant! She would be the introduction to the "Cunt" monologue, and I knew she would do an excellent job.

There were still some setbacks, because I wanted Marissa to be more and more involved in the show. She had a voice and a story that *needed* to be heard.

Copyright and legal issues made it impossible for this to happen, and my heart was broken again and again throughout the journey of putting on the show. I knew her heart was broken many times too, but she was always so patient with me. I wish I could have done so much more, but she was so understanding regardless.

Her compassion spread out in other ways as well. She's an amazing person and friend, and I appreciated her support more than I can describe. She made me laugh when I did her makeup, and she held me when I was sobbing while telling my own story. She could feel my heartache and did exactly what I needed in my moment of pain.

She comforted me and let me know that she was a rock I could lean on to get through the rough times. Even if distance separated us, I knew she would forever be someone I could reach out to who would listen to and support me and love me.

Marissa never ceased being amazing. Not only is she an incredible woman and friend, but she was also an inspiration to thousands of people who came to watch *The Vagina Monologues*.

Marissa's presence on the stage was breathtaking. She commanded the attention of the entire audience. She was so brave. This was her first time performing as the person she is, and I was living for it. She was bringing life to the entire auditorium, and I was so proud to see all the obstacles she's overcome manifesting in a powerful moment of defiance, solidarity, and unbreakable strength.

Marissa sometimes thanks me for the opportunity I have given her. I really don't understand this, though. I feel like she has given me so much more than I could ever repay her for. I am grateful to call her my friend, and honored that she would even include me in this amazing project.

Marissa, I hope you know that I love you. I hope you know that I am so proud of you and that I admire you so much. You are such a special person. Thank you for continuing to inspire me and those around you.

AUTHOR'S NOTE: AT THE RISK OF THIS PIECE SOUNDING self-congratulatory or indulgent, I just wanted to mention that this is what Pearl chose to write in the spirit of this book. I did not ask her to write a piece about me, in case it came across that way. Thank you.

❧ 6 ❧

PIXIE DUST AND STAR STUFF

by Marissa Alexa McCool

Spotlight
Stage right
Low dim
Turn up the gain
Fix my lipstick offset by four cups of coffee
Darling
Give me a blue light for the third act
Sparkle

Main
My Center
My arm
My beating heart
Eyes glinting in the fervor of serving the servicer
Smoke
Sentiment
Sentience

Mania with a twist of rose-colored nostalgia and a
    dash of modernist hope
Mix well
Two tracks

Break
Illumination Theory
Set
Blonde mohawk
Hidden secrets
Peeling layers
Answers to the questions achingly repressed from
    the external inquisitors
Conquistadores
Silence by agency denial
Storm

Dance
Uneven even flow
Broken looking glass mirror
Act 4 but with the sex edited out for cable
Four left feet
Two shimmering smiles
One beating heart
Spin me like my Vyvanse
Catch me like a broken fall
Bind me like handfasting
I'm a knot
Your unseverable ties
Downpour

Spotlight

Stage rear
Forced perspective
Look down to look up
Speak to be silenced
Stare to be challenged
Quench the permission for lust
Needs more gay
Use the act of nature to commit the entrancing of
    eternity
Becoming one
Satiate the insatiable
Repeat
Delivery confirmation
Signature required
Initial on the dotted hip
Bottom copy's yours
Sleep on it
Pixie Dust

Curtains
Encore
Take a bow
Grasp the hand
Never let me go
Renew the lease
Rent to own
Retrace the steps
Say the words
Hypnotize the cues
Follow the lights
Let go to hold closer
There you are

There we are
Again
For now
For all
For ever

7

MY MARK ONE IS JEALOUS

by Bethany Futrell

HERE'S THE THING—MY MARK ONE IS STANDARD ISSUE: a perfectly normal vagina. Sure, we're friends and all. We do the hand-mirror-hang-out regularly. I like making her happy, and she likes it too. We both like visits by our partner, and we have been content for a very long time.

Lately, however, she's been dissatisfied with herself. I have tried to explain to her that she's beautiful just the way she is, and she doesn't need to change a thing. My partner tells her she is wonderful. I have spent evenings (and mornings) comforting her, but it seems nothing will change her mind. She's jealous.

Since she learned of shiny new science vaginas, my Mark One feels left out. *Why can't we be shiny and new?* she asks me, and I struggle to help her understand.

We were born this way, I say, *and there are other people who were not born this way, though they should have been.*

There are women everywhere who were born with other pieces that just don't match up, and they need the option to be confirmed—just like we were at birth. Other women need to be able to choose to have a companion just like I have had in her my whole life.

No matter how I explain it, she still doesn't understand. *They will be newer and better,* she tells me. *They will be perfect, and we will not.*

But you are perfect, I respond each time. *You are perfect, and you just don't understand. We won the genetic lottery! I got to have you in my life from the moment I was born, and I have loved every moment with you.*

And yet even though she has never actually seen a shiny new science vagina, she just *knows* they're better than she is. They're technologically improved, built by loving hands, and she was just formed in a womb by some chemicals. The tech has to make them better, does it not?

Oh, sweet Mark One, of course not. Just because they are shiny and new does not mean they are better or worse. It means they are the same. That is why the surgery exists! Because inside, these women are the same as we are, and they deserve the chance to be the same outside too.

They should be confirmed as who they are just like we are every day. They should not be discriminated against by potential partners or governments or business owners or employers or anyone. They are the same, not better or worse. Beautiful women everywhere, just like us, who deserve love and homes and jobs and friendship—they are shiny and wonderful, just as we are.

Don't you want them to feel shiny and wonderful? Don't you want them to feel affirmed? Shouldn't they get to choose the options which make them feel *right*?

They are our friends and family members. They are our

partners and loved ones. They are just like us, and their shiny new science vaginas are just like you, Mark One.

But hell if I can convince her.

8

ONCE UNSPOKEN

2017

by Marissa Alexa McCool

To the world, I'm 31. To myself, I'm 13.
13 years ago, that's when I got my name.
The name that would stick in my mind,
The name I would crave to be called,
The name that made me cry at night,
The name that made me wish it'd gone away,
That was the name that stayed in my heart.

A drag queen is what I thought I was,
Because I didn't know any better.
We weren't educated on such things.
Even the open-minded among us,
To our groups, conversations, and movies,
Trans people existed only as
Jokes
Punchlines

Comedy
Fodder
Plot twists.
That was all we knew.

"Drag queen" is what I let them call me,
To pretend that I was laughing with them,
Instead of believing the laughter was at me.
But I loved the makeup, the clothes, the shoes,
The way my eyes looked with mascara,
The way my legs felt smooth to the touch,
The way I felt unapologetically myself,
And nobody could take that from me.

But I had to keep it a secret.
It was too much for some people to handle.
They thought I should be a real man,
Be a provider, protector, breadwinner,
The cuddler, the kisser, the initiator,
Even those who said they understood,
Appreciated the dynamic,
Thought it was kinda hot,
Always defaulted to the traditional expectation.
Too emotional, too needy, too affectionate,
"Stop trying to be the little spoon!"
"Stop being scared at loud noises!"
"Stop wearing such bright colors!"
"Stop skipping, stop dancing, stop singing,
Stop wearing eyeliner, stop tilting your head,
Stop putting your hand on your hip,
Stop being so...
Girly!"

Growing up pretending to be a boy,
Girly was the worst thing you could be.
You play like a girl, you cry like a girl,
You were a pussy if you were weak,
You were a girlfriend if you didn't like guns,
Girls couldn't rape guys because,
Huh-huh, you can't rape the willing, LOL, right?
Hey baby, you don't need the gun!
High-five, bro!

I craved to be protected.
I adored feeling like people wanted
To stand up for me
To let me cry
To let them be there for me,
But I couldn't.
I wasn't being honest with myself
Because I was scared.
Terrified.
What would the world think?
What would my parents think?
What would happen to me?
Would I be bullied?
Beaten?
Assaulted?
Killed?

Then I found the Queer Dictionary.
I read through the words, the labels, the definitions.
I wasn't a drag queen.
I wasn't a crossdresser.
Transgender though, that seemed right.
But it was too much commitment.

So I went with gender queer,
Non-binary,
Genderfluid,
Gender nonconforming...
Anything that allowed me to be Marissa,
But not take the full jump.
No hormones, no shots, no meds,
Nothing permanent.
Permanent was scary.

However, as I became Marissa,
I stopped liking being called sir.
I began to hate my deadname.
I began to hate being associated as a guy,
A male,
A him,
A dude,
A bro,
Thank you very much, sir.
Have a nice day, sir.
Is this your husband?
Is this your father?

I wanted to be one of the girls.
I wanted to be a girl.
I... am a girl.
I couldn't even commit to it when I went on HRT,
But my spouse referred to me as Marissa,
Ris,
Rissy Monster,
Princess,
Baby.
He called me beautiful, precious,

Pretty, princess, baby girl...
All the things I wanted to be called my entire life,
But wasn't allowed.
Cause that'd be gay, right?

But then...
Then two people took from me.
Like thieves in the night, they stole.
They took my body.
They took my rights.
They took my voice.
They took
My consent.
I hid.
I ran.
I fled.
I became numb.
Distant.
Vacant.
I cut my hair.
Ditched outfits.
Tossed aside the makeup.
Died inside every time someone called me
    <deadname>,
But I dealt with it.
Because that's what the world was like
To people like me
If I was true.

Then one day, he came to our school.
Pastor Carl.
Filled with hate,
Bigotry,

Moral superiority,
Slurs,
Threats,
Damnation,
Scare-tactics,
Humiliation,
And self-righteousness.
He called girls sluts,
Gay people words I won't repeat,
And trans acceptance was the reason
Penn had a suicide problem.
Not because of bullies like him,
But because being who we are
Was subconscious defiance of truth.
That's why we hurt,
That's why we suffered,
That's why we died,
Because Pastor Carl knew the truth
And we ran from it.
We only chose to be who we were
To mock God.

As I stood up to him,
I was no longer afraid.
Nothing he said could touch me.
Nothing he said could penetrate my shield.
Nothing he said mattered.
So I yelled directly in his face:
"I'm transgender, fuck you!"
And that was it.
I was out.
I was Marissa.

Then we got a new president
And all hell broke loose.
The same fear I'd had for years,
Seemed to consume the many.
So I wrote,
Yelled,
Podcasted,
Published,
Guested,
Stood up,
Stood out,
Owned who I was,
And within three months,
I was Marissa-fuckin'-McCool.
Published author,
LGBT columnist,
Trans podcaster,
Guest on *God Awful Movies*,
And now, performing in *The Vagina Monologues*.
As me.
As Marissa.
As Marissa Alexa McCool.
Who I've always been.
True.

Tonight is not my first, or even hundredth
Time on stage in public,
But it is the first time,
The very first time,
That any cast list or program
Will read: Marissa Alexa McCool.
And that, my dear friends,
Was worth every step of the journey.

9

SIR: JUST A WORD TO YOU

by Marissa Alexa McCool

Have a good day, sir
May I help you, sir?
How are you, sir?
Good day, sir

The onus is on me
To always correct you
Never on you
To get it right

Thank you, sir
Excuse me, sir
Is that all, sir?
What do you mean it's not "sir"?

I have to present myself

58

In a way that makes
You not have to judge
Based on my height
Or me wanting to
Not have to wear
Makeup that day

Sometimes that doesn't work, either
In a full dress
With makeup
On Delta Airlines
Or at my own job
With a boss
Who has only known me
As me
Yet still lets
One slip
Every now and then

A cis woman
Is still a woman
In sweatpants or a T-shirt
And so am I
I don't become a sir
Once I use
Makeup remover
Or dress casually

I am who I am
And I will correct you
I'm not a sir
In parentheses
Goddammit

Why does that need
To be gendered, anyway?
Isn't "how may I help you"
Polite enough
Without a gendered
Salutation?

But leave room for mistakes
Everybody messes up
You weren't in makeup
What did you expect?
There's always a reason
That I should let it go
When I have the nerve
To make someone
Uncomfortable
Because I was hurt
By them being
Wrong

I
Am
Not
A
Fucking
Sir!

10

LINES ON HER BODY

by Anonymous K

"I'm going to give you something you've never had before, and I promise, you're going to like it."

The words rolled off his tongue as his hot breath gusted against her neck.

She remembers feeling the total presence of someone else invading her body. Her chaste eyes stared at the industrial piping, too afraid of tainting her mind by watching him pumping the innocence from her body. In the browning basement of the local Packers apparel retailer, her head rocked against rotting shipping boxes, a hard mass jutting recklessly inside her body, tearing at her skin as blood softened the feeling of him forcing himself inside.

That day, this man—almost 10 years her senior—became more aware of her 14-year-old body than she had ever been or will ever be. She has never been that close to herself, and 13 years later, she's left wondering if she'll ever know her own skin as intimately as he did, angrily hissing to her that if she screamed, he'd stop her, and it would hurt. As if what he was doing didn't hurt so much that she stopped feeling altogether.

Since she was nine years old, the world outside of her eyes was untouchable. Back then, she didn't know that when she moved through air, down streets, others saw her. She's never seen herself, and so when her hands dip into the light, block her gaze, she wonders whose hands could be so scarred, so bruised, when she knows they're only 27 years old.

There is no feeling inside her body. She keeps looking for someone to make her feel alive inside. But giving someone feelings is harder than shoving your body inside of them, which is what most people want.

Outside, she feels pain, but that feels like life—and so it is good. It started with scratches and pinches and small burns. But when her heart filled with the unspeakable, untouchable emptiness that pierces an eternal soul with the confinement of temporal reality, the scratches became a complete separation of epithelium.

At first the dewy blood formed droplets on her skin, but she needed to know she was alive. Deeper cuts. Fresh erythrocytes trickled down supple thighs like a mother's soft, tickling hands as she lulls her baby to sleep.

But she is not a baby, and she continued to cut.

What would she tell her baby someday? Back then, she didn't know that her baby would never come. Back then, she didn't know that the cut precipitating down her arm was the most natural thing her body would ever reproduce.

Soon, her desires turned to art. Now she is covered in flowers and words where scars leave rifts in her skin, provoking unwanted questions from meddlesome voyeurs.

But nobody thinks to ask anymore, anyway.

Her mother refers to the day she married her first husband as "that day you were so beautiful and nothing in particular happened." But that isn't clever or funny, because that was the day she promised herself to the man who spent the next 18 months hitting, bruising, raping, and removing any vision she had of herself as whole, unbroken. Even though he left her body damaged and empty, he is important to her because he has the stolen debris of the girl who came to him, broken and searching for anything.

Heaviness
laces the structure of her bones
burning coldly as each bodily memory
reverberates with
touching, caressing,
memories, burning like the sins of youth,
sending her back to the nightly Hell
where she watches herself endlessly

Panic
emerges inside her head,
neurons calibrated and ready to fire:
he appears in her mind whenever she is touched.
But there are so many hims.
And she sees each one,
with every stroke of skin, it takes her away from now
away from her.
Wrists pulling her down,
someone else's flesh absorbing hers—

What is it for?

What is she for?
Who is she for?

People speak of memories as if they are waves,
sometimes floods,
or fragments.
But her memories are sharp
like fire and blood.
They don't come in floods
or waves
and the fragments
speak to her ears in broken English—
memories confuse her dreams.

From the slightest inclination,
they sneak up
preying on ecstasy,
crushing like anvils in prolonged
unbreakable
unleavable
spaces.

Making her completely aware of what's happening
again and again.
They tell her to leave,
because she's not really there. But she is there,
reliving her departure,
from a former self.

They all took pieces of her
replacing it with a little bit of them,
so, no matter how alone, secluded, reclusive
she keeps her body,

when touched
her mental activities
and passivities,
of which she is completely unconscious,
manifest their existence by effects that
consume her.

By now her eyes are gone.
Can you hear her memories too?
"Hush, you are here. With me."
Loving words breathe into her,
inhaling the panic and fear
quivering below the surface of her psyche...

Her cheeks fit perfectly in the crux of your
neck, steeped in patchouli and juniper breeze.
When she is with you, she is
Home.
The smell of your skin
lingers in her mouth.
Vegetation from summer bursts between her lips
and the flavor of salt stings with warm tang
the tongue that has swallowed more than tears.
When you kiss her,
she drinks mouthfuls of your history.
And she knows herself,
as she is known.

BUT HE WASN'T THE ONLY ONE. AFTER THAT, MEN
began routinely invading her body—violently, manipula-
tively, with presumed authority granted to them by her

family and society, in a variety of ways and places with an entire cast of fools, and they left wounds, internal and external, that she carries in secret.

Back then, this girl was a child. At 18, we never know who we are—even though we are very sure. This girl was no different.

I know because she is me—I am her. But writing this story from my own perspective is hard because I don't really know who I am. How can I really know when my perception of myself—what I do, how I do it, what I look like— doesn't ever form the same image as the one I am given?

People tell me about myself, and I learn. I don't know how to look at myself and know who I am.

And now my story comes in cycles, where I can't really remember which parts connect to others, because my body knows things about myself that I can't even comprehend.

When a breath of wind approaches one of my body's secret places—a place I forgot that he repossessed, scratching bits of my youthful epithelium—a shiver of memory pulses so violently through my bones that I think he's actually behind me, waiting to close my neck between his fists until I am allowed to refill my lungs.

The fact of the matter is, that the time he held me down in the basement of that smutty store didn't destroy me. It was being alone in that big fucking house destroyed me.

As the family of a Reformed Baptist minister, my family lived in a parsonage. The church touched our backyard, so naturally, the weight of life, death, and our souls' eternal resting place infiltrated every aspect of our lives. How a young woman should act, what she should do to protect herself from defilement, the modes, methods, and perfections of innocence and virginity consumed every message in my world.

As a nine-year-old, I remember thinking about my sister's life as totally separate from my own. Slowly skipping in the drenching Indianan sun on the cracked and grainy sidewalk, with unevenly placed blocks which connected my back door with the church's, my mind tried to conceptualize another reality where I wasn't myself.

The realization that every moment I experience imprints uniquely in my mind and consciousness burns into my soul. I tried to think about being someone else, somewhere else, but in that moment, I realized that my body housed my reality, and no matter how badly I wished it so, I could never be anyone else or start at another point in time; this was my only life.

The weight of this responsibility wore my conscious thin, and my skin began to break out, and my heart began to fall apart any time my actions reflected poorly on the beliefs which imbued my worldview.

The next year, we moved north, the farthest north any of us had been. I'll never forget the *Star Wars*-pattern of the night sky as we drove through the meandering backwoods path through Cable, Wisconsin on our first visit to the dismal shithole from which I would later emerge a mentally dysmorphic wreck.

Moving to a coppice town taught me something about physical contact I never learned from the quiet Chicagoan suburb, where the only bully was a dog.

Boys play rough in the woods. By the time I was 12 years old, my body knew the torment of someone bigger and stronger—I had been tackled, pinned, shoved, tied down, shot at, and locked up so many times that anything else felt like a dereliction.

And by 13, I began actively participating in the defilement of my body. As if it was yesterday, I remember taking the first slit at my wrists after a particularly nasty fight between me and my mom—she accused me of stealing and losing her scissors. Feeling the inhuman trespassing on my castrated human shell, mingling metal and blood, leaving a permanent mark in my flesh, gave me a supreme control.

It was not a full 12 months later when the first man forced me to feel that being a woman meant relinquishing control.

He kept telling me that I wanted it. Why did I believe him? Why do I still struggle to disagree with him? If someone told me this story, I would have no problem assuring them that they did not have any responsibility in the act.

It wasn't even until several months after the first time that I realized my body was keeping secrets. I had started the newest season of *Gilmore Girls*, and in one nauseating moment, the actor who plays Luke flashed his penetrating almond-butter eyes at the screen and my stomach took control. Within seconds, I was vomiting, his face cast on the screen of my pursed eyelids.

I couldn't believe what I had done. That's what I remember feeling—thinking. *What have I done?*

The next time it happened, I wasn't much older. 16 now, same location—the dismal Packers storefront caked with snow crystals. My key popped the latch, and we slipped through the threshold. How could I be such an idiot? Alone again with a boy at 6:00 a.m. in downtown Hayward, Wisconsin during the middle of October. Death doesn't know a stricter silence than those empty village streets.

He made me feel dangerous. He watched professional wrestling and wore the same Spencer's fishnets as me. Finding a kindred spirit in that rural Wisconsin wasteland felt like a gift—until he was holding me by the back of my neck, telling me that I could breathe when he finished.

My tongue adapted—my mouth learning tricks that my brain cannot conjugate. But my body knows.

After he finished, his leather hands, gritty with earth and manhood, cusped my mouth—forcing me to taste him in the back of my throat while he gluttonously welcomed me to re-perform for him whenever I wanted.

Just like the first time, this him made me believe I wanted it. Feeling like I wanted him made me hate my body for being so empty that men constantly were able to fill it up.

In those days, I cut myself daily. Like, *really fucking daily*. I had to feel something before I could feel anything. It was my coffee, except it woke up the nagging voice that threatened me with eternal loneliness and damnation at the hand of an angry God (although my God was not angry at me).

I didn't know why I felt so afraid of my own thoughts, my mind constantly screaming, my heart unsure of who I was or where to find solace from the empty clattering that choked my heart, causing massive anxiety and self-doubt.

The voice kept me company; and by detaching myself from it, I could pretend I wasn't alone.

Alone. That is how I feel in here, my body. It isn't a matter of whether I know who I am, but rather, who I am feels like a visitor—a stranger—in my own body.

That voice conducted me. It fueled the strangeness I felt, my body being torched by puberty, self-induced blood-letting, and the constant fear that, without a man to absorb me, I had no purpose.

When I married my husband, it had been two years since second rape. He drove around the guy's house with a baseball bat, just waiting for him to come outside. Immaturity found this potently romantic, and every bone in my body belonged to him. And he knew that.

My house was so big. Like a princess locked away in a castle, he kissed me in the morning as I sat at our kitchen table with a pot of black coffee and a cigarette. I was so thin in those days. All I ate was tomato soup and toast—we couldn't afford much more, but the gardens were vibrant in the spring, so then we ate lettuce and cucumbers, pickling the rest with the warmth of my mother's secret recipe.

Though I was weak, I was not fragile. Every day he would work from 6:00 a.m. to 6:00 p.m.—I thought he was working, anyway. And while he worked, I scrubbed our house from top to bottom. That fucking house, full of demons that steal cats and watch you while you dream, hoping you can feel their puncturing eyes.

In the morning, he left for work, and I would spend roughly 30-60 minutes with one of my best friends: *Frasier, Get Smart, I Love Lucy, The Andy Griffith Show, The Cosby Show,* Dick Van Dyke, or Mary Tyler Moore. Oh, and Bob Newhart.

Two cups of coffee, and then it was time to domesticate. Fill the red bucket with hot, soapy water. Add a little lavender in the spring (to repel spiders) and a little lemon dish soap to help with gnats and fruit flies. Always start at the top; wipe down every cupboard and cabinet, all the chairs, stools, and door frames, the mantel and wood-panel walls, banisters, steps, and trim.

A cigarette. Then dust all the knickknacks—Bibles, snow globes, china tea sets, tiny glass kittens, lighthouses—and rearrange anything that looks stale.

Another cigarette. Use the hand-vac for all corners,

fabric chairs, pillows, sofas, curtains (except every other day, wash the curtains), and stuffed animals.

Meanwhile, wash the towels—rotate bi-daily kitchen towels and bath towels.

Once all the wood is dry, sweep and mop the floors—bathroom floors are done by hand to ensure each crevice has been scrubbed.

Another cigarette. The final stage: vacuuming, top to bottom, the whole 3,000 square feet takes roughly an hour.

That house was my body, and with my body, I maintained it so that every day he could come home, always a little drunker than when he left, hold me down on my polished linoleum, and force himself inside of me before I could even say hello. It was his way of keeping me in the house, because every morning, I just needed to clean—purge the night.

When he left, it was the worst and best day of my life. I remember running down the street after him because it was the first day I'd breached the property line in over six months.

That was 10 years ago.

Now I live my life, not unhappy, but not as a whole person. All the men who visited—invaded—took pieces like souvenirs; they colonized my body with ditches and ridges that cannot be removed.

So what am I, if not broken? A whole identity locked in a fractured cage.

I don't have an ending to this story. For now, I see through a mirror, and it is so fucking dark. But one day, I will see face to face. And I will be known as I am known.

Today, I am not perfect, because being perfect means being done, and I know I'm not done. And though it doesn't feel like it now, I won't be broken forever.

❧ II ❧

I'VE TRAVELED

by Marissa Alexa McCool

I've traveled through iron ridges
Wind farms on the freeway
Dissociation trips
And along the great rocks
Trying to get my best look
At the eyes
That render me helpless

I've traveled through states
That legislate against me
Going stealth to be safe
Hiding who I am
To get to where you are
So you can see me
As I truly am

I've traveled through space
Hidden memories and desires
I never again thought I'd visit
And new ones upon which
You've shined a first light
And made first glance
Into a world full of
New definitions

I've traveled throughout the country
Searching for the love
Of a woman
Hoping that one day
She'd make me as happy
As I could ever hope to be
And yet, there she was
In the last place I was expecting
With all the rules ready

I've traveled with her hand
Grasping mine, fearing goodbye
Counting down before we leave
Wondering where the next will be
Hoping against hope
Dying for closeness
Aching for reprieve
Needing that moment
Where we're both
Safe again

I've traveled through mindspace
And now I'm in subspace, littlespace
But none more important

Than the space we've created
Our own little world
That makes Grand Marais
A mere postcard by comparison
Where I'll be a bride
She'll be the only scenery
I need to worry about seeing
First, and
Only

12

ODE TO THE BLOCKED—BEFORE YOU COULD BLOCK

by Marissa Alexa McCool
and
Emmalia Petra Fae George
"Ris n' Priss"

STOP BEING SUCH A PROFESSIONAL VICTIM.
Stop being such a professional dreamer.
I hate my waistline.
I hate my shoulders.
Why can't I be a little thinner?
Why am I so tall?
What's stopping me from just going to the store and wasting money right now on things I don't need like food?
What's stopping me from impulsively buying a plane ticket I can't afford to somewhere I've never been to meet someone I've never met?
You better not listen to too much of that style of music,

someone's going to think you're some pot-smoking hippie or worse, a liberal.

You better like the music and sports that I do, otherwise you're gonna keep getting called a fag at school.

You wear too much black.

You wear makeup.

Why don't you smile more?

Why don't you look like you're having fun?

Why do I want the pink bottle of stuff to shave instead of the red one?

Why do you shave your legs? That's gross.

Why are you a lesbian?

Why can't you just be gay?

Why don't you like boys?

Why aren't you like the other boys?

Boys can take care of you, and plus they really are better at figuring stuff out than us girls, so why don't you want one in your life?

We've always known this about you. Why don't you just admit it?

Why do you spend so much time in the kitchen with mommy? Your brother and dad are in there so go spend time with them while I clean up the kitchen

All these women talk about how sexy your eyelashes are. But don't let that go to your head. You're not actually a woman. You just make them jealous.

Oh you don't want to watch the game? Then we'll go to bed early and sleep just like this in our bed.

You look old enough. No one will ever have to know.

❧

IN THE MORNINGS, MY MOTHER WOULD GENTLY WAKE ME up and carry me across the house to her room, where she'd lay me on her bed while Dad was showering and getting ready for work. Then my mom would go make breakfast. After she was done, she'd dress me. I mean pick out my clothes and put them on me.

They did this until the middle of fifth grade when I kicked my mother in the face when she was trying to do it. I never really thought about why I was struggling with her at the time. I just thought I was being a shitty, bratty kid. But now I'm older and I know that nine-year-olds don't get dressed by their mother, and...

No, they don't. And these were moments you didn't think of at the time because it was the only normal you knew. Reflection once you've escaped the bubble can be the scariest thing in the world. Take it from someone who is also in love with someone who was raised in a cult. They told me a story on the way home about how they couldn't afford lice shampoo, so they had to use WD-40 on the hair they were never allowed to cut.

It's actually kind of interesting. I feel like an archaeologist.

That's a great metaphor, because that's literally what archaeologists and anthropologists did initially. They were people who wanted to understand "primitive" societies. Then it turned out those people were also actually people, and the discipline had to evolve from "why do certain people do this thing?" to "why don't I ask why this is happening and I have a problem with it?" to "what really happened to me that is making me uncomfortable?

WHAT'S THE POINT OF WANTING TO BE A WOMAN IF you're just going to sleep with other women?

Of course, because women's primary function in the world is to be desirable and fuckable by men. In what other context could the "Friend Zone" exist?

৯৯

WHY ARE YOU SAD?

Why do you look so bored?

How hard is it to just be in a better mood?

Nobody's going to pick you if they think you don't care.

You want to feel better, right?

People judge you by the way you look.

So then stop feeling fucking sorry for yourself and stand up.

Start living up to your potential that we've defined.

Man up.

Don't be gay.

Fight it.

Be a man.

Fight back.

Do it, pussy!

Oh, you're going to use something other than your fists? That's cute.

Wait, you actually hurt someone!

Don't make fun of yourself.

Did you break that guy's wrist?

We're not laughing with you.

That wasn't funny.

You're the joke.

You're the crazy one. You should be in the hospital.

WHY DO YOU TAKE SO MANY MEDS?

You won't be able to leave football practice for headaches.

You're like your mother-in-law. She's had electroshock therapy.

Migraines aren't any excuse to completely pass out. We thought you were drunk that time when you were 15 and had to be literally carried into the house. That's how much we thought of you at the time.

I bet she was just really bored and needed excitement in her life.

It's much easier to think how messed up you must be than it is to consider our role in it.

ALL OF THIS HURTS SO MUCH. I FEEL LIKE I'M GETTING pulled down some hole in the ground. I can't breathe and everything touching me is so fucking coarse, and I want out of here but it won't let me go.

Sometimes when I'm in that hole, I go to the place I was at my most vulnerable. When I was running away. When I was being raped. When I was locked in a room and not allowed to use the bathroom. It all comes back to me.

I am mortified that I will use all of this, all of these feelings, as an excuse to run away and hide, to detransition, to leave the Earth, to leave it, whatever that means.

Hiding isn't entirely bad, but I won't let you run away. We all need time and space, but we promised every day we have to each other, and I can't and won't let you do that. I know who you are, and I will protect you as much as you protect me. You are Priss. No detransitioning. Or, if it's what it takes, I'll detransition with you. Just like I'd jump into a lake of fire to pull you back out. You go, I go. That's how this works.

Okay. I understand how saying that must have hurt. I'm sorry.

No, no apologies. Yes it hurts, but that's part of the deal that's you, that's us. We hurt, and we have years of trauma that we're still unpacking. It's going to hurt, it has to. You feel what I feel, and I feel what you feel. We're in this together, and that means the bad parts too.

๛

WHAT IF IT'S TOO MUCH? I KNOW YOU DON'T BREAK, BUT I don't want you bent.

You're worth it, even if I do break. I've put myself back together before. I can handle it.

This is far too fucking long.

No—I mean the time we have to wait.

Yes. That is true. It's the longing of an addiction combined with the void of the euphoria I only get when you're around.

My wrists hurt and there's only two people in the world I can tell.

I think I'm going deaf and I am so, so scared.

I'm here, no matter what. If you're going deaf, I'll help you adjust. Whatever it is, we will deal with it, and I am there walking beside you, with you, your hand in mine, every step of the way.

I WILL DO THAT WITH YOU. I PROMISE.

I believe you.

The best part of a truth is that it is real. I don't have to believe it.

You don't have to. Of course you don't. But it doesn't mean I'm going to stop reminding you. It doesn't mean I'm going to stop telling you, even if it is so freaking obvious that it's tattooed on your forehead. I will still tell you. The most dangerous thought in this world is that someone already knows how you feel, or what you feel. I will never let that happen with you.

Are you sure you can keep that promise?

What did you just say about a truth?

I understand. Touché.

WE'RE SO FUCKED. AREN'T WE? LIKE, IN THE GOOD WAY?

Yep. Since day one.

So now what?

We work toward both our short-term and long-term goals. Sometimes we self-care. Sometimes we hide. Sometimes we need to cry. But even by doing that, we're still working toward our goals. Short-term—podcast tonight. Not so short-term—how long until I see you. Long-term—you know exactly what that means.

I do.

I do.

13

THE IMPOSSIBLE BLUE SKY

by Emmalia Petra Fae George

The sky is blue.
The wind beyond my window is calling my name.
Drawing out the all the s's like a self-eating snake
And I am sitting here and looking through it
    remembering that one day
In Smyrna
where the sky was impossibly blue and those two
    girls wanted you to stay
And their room held that same hue
the impossible blue
One of wonder
One of new things to come

I watched with a fascination.
They were so utterly happy. Content.
So sharply it changed

Outside was level and boring and this room was a
    rollercoaster and I was on a gradient
Taking me far and above the Earth, showing me
    everything
All at once and since I'm only human, the universe
    gave me the right eyes to see it.
All at once the future becomes clear, that for the
    next 25 years
I will have to hide this knowing inside while I'm
    growing
away reluctantly holding this destructive chemical
    that will turn me into a boy

But oh, how it would feel to feel, to feel like them
To truly be worthy. Truly be seen
Because testosterone is monochrome and estrogen's
    a plasma screen
And when you turn me on *goddamn* that pixel
    density
This is it
This is it
The only missing puzzle piece.

But it would take those 25 years to slide it back
    into frame
Laser-cut out of life and my name with such expert
    precision
That no one will ever know the difference
But for now sister-girl, you get to stew and
    worry away inside this monkey-suit of
    a shell
And watch on TV those girls like those girls you
    that you though you knew so well

Until that one day when the puzzle slipped apart
    and the walls fell

They fell so hard that the only place you could go is
    a step on the way to get back
Into the arms of those little girls under that
    impossible blue
where you first thought that dress might look a little
    better on you

And at Rachel's 16th birthday party, you'd find out
    that was true
And later when the horrible one—
Yes, it's time to mention her

When the horrible one saw you and opened up her
    jaws to spit
What a good girl you've been
You felt empowered instead of scared
She wanted you scared

She lost.

Fast forward the VHS tape of your memories
Get to where you are now.
Back to the room colored like a dark wine
Back to the glass, the purple lipstick and the pickle
    brine
By your fingertips diluting with time, growing
    calluses
like when you played your first guitar
Back to the world in which the cat has died

And your brain screams about patterns and re-
    learning how to write
Back to the medication you just took and how it's
    slowing your reaction time
Who Cares? Anyway your priorities are ducks in a
    single fucking line
And it doesn't matter how you feel right now
    because you're
On top of things like those hearts weigh on top
    of you.
They hold you so close.
Time to hold them back.

Back to the window. The trees are so very much
    taller now
But you are so, so brave. You learned to look past
    them and see yourself within the blue, the
    perfect impossible blue and then you can
finally

finally

smile.

How arrogant of you.
Do you really believe that commodifying your
    opinion is going to lead you to success? How
    dare you?
How dare you stare out at this impossibly blue sky
    and not disintegrate under the weight of
    hunger?
You are better than that, you deserve to die on the
    cross of your privilege

How dare I? Like this.
Like the only way I know how
Like when mister B in the third grade
Told me that my words were clay
And to form them
While the other kids had to write a presentation to
    give the class
He would give me a sheet with a small Calvin and
    Hobbes drawing he found
And ask me to write a story and in an hour I had
    four pages written
With no sign of slowing down
It's quite a lot for an eight-year-old.

So maybe that should really be the goal
For me to put these pieces together until they
    become the whole

And to describe my loves. Because they each
    deserve to be known
They are my reason for waking up
They are my everything
Instead of finding excuses to stay in bed
I spend an hour thinking of what I will do once I
    get out

My loves, you have turned me into an optimist
My glass is not half-empty or half-full
It is filled to the brim three times over
And I will drink it down every day
Because we all know how important it is to keep
    hydrated

I am here to describe my life because it is comprised
    of other amazing people
I am an altruist, existing to translate and give back
Running far beyond the gray hills of becoming an
    empath

And this is my diary.

And no matter how much I keep writing I will
    never move past the immediacy of the
    first page.

A month ago, you met me for coffee and intended to
    talk about one specific thing
Instead we spent two hours learning each other's'
    names
I don't have patience for much left in this world
But the way you explain things keeps me riveted to
    the floor
Stimulating every nerve and pore
And your eyes, I know what they mean.
You use every word you can, except that one
I know you're still fumbling for your keys here
But we all are.
And this is all at once.
But we will continue to learn

Your willingness to give seems to never be able
    to stop
So much that your ex left because she was waiting
    for the bad shoe to drop
And it's her loss, because I know it never will

But if it were, you know you wouldn't be here and
     you wouldn't want that anyway
Because baby
you are the wind
Encouraging me at my back and looking deep
     within

I looked outside at you and there by the glow of
     your phone
Was the chiseled-in-the-best-way-possible outline of
     your face.
The glow was staring at you intensely and
     smoking
From the menthol on your lips
You didn't know that I know and I always have.
You're pushing Facebook down the street
concerned about where you'll be
and what it means now that people might see you.
Your cigarette is everything for a flash and I
     remember so much
through my saccharin prism of marijuana and lady
     grey tea.
This moment that I watched you have alone made
     me shiver.
There is no embrace like this.
They just can't exist

What I wouldn't give to see you on that stage
     some night
Slithering your hips and jettisoning your stage
     fright.
We'll get there, sweetie.
But for now, hold tight.

I am laying here and you are crawling in through
    the windows and it is your touch.
You are a superhero
So many miles away and yet and I can feel you
Your optimistic warmth is late spring in the
    north and
I am basking in the first hints of your summer.
And this is how I wake up each morning

You lovingly reassure me that you are mine and I
    am yours and it is whole.
And this is further magnified when your thoughts
    push me to the floor
And my phone rings one last time with the words
    "goodnight sweet metamour"
And compersion is real, and it is glorious.
Go ahead and play that song, sweetie, it's already
    ruined by us.

And like that you lay down in the west.
You change into the little one who I love just as if
    she were here in front of me
And that's because she is
I see her.
You change into the little one
Who I wonder
How is it possible
That something so precious exists.
Your silent auction has no end
We just keep climbing in the numbers until the
    atmosphere distends and melts
and ultimately, we conclude humanity has no hand

in calculating your worth.
You are so unilaterally good natured that you
    redefine the words.
You are the honeysuckle creeping through the fence
    in first grade.
You are the author.
You may exist because of trauma and hate
and I would never wish that on the worst of the
    world, but I am lucky still
Because inside you there are two amazing people
    instead of one
Which means I get to wrap myself up in twice the
    love here.
Baby, you are the sun.

You say you're north of me.
But when the morning comes and you look back at
    where you've been
I'll look due east, basking in your rays again.
We'll be together soon.
Because you're also the moon.

For someone who's got something to say about
    everything
I find it hard as fuck to cobble together words when
    it comes to you.
Even though you've never said it
You regret that I've not written much about us.
But the truth is there is no way to do it.
When I start to tell people who I am
I tell them who you are—and when they try to
    correct me
I correct them and say

No! You can't know.
You don't get to know what we are
because if you'll just let me explain.
Then you'll get a glimpse of her rain.
Her words hit the pavement harsh
And yes, she makes me so mad sometimes
but at the end of the day I am always a puddle and
Goddamn, does she ever drink me up from the
    asphalt.

I write nothing because there is no description
For when she and I sink into a freshly made bed.
And although I'm tall and want a king-size
A little part of me will always hate that we have the
    option to be further apart.

We can share so much with a single look.
We are shorthand, knowing more fully than
    anything else.

When I say the word "Corbin," you know what
    that means
When I play Aerosmith you know what that means
When we buy three copies of the Everglow by Mae
Because we don't want a single day
To pass without seeing it in the frame
across from that little sheet of paper that Blair
    signed signifying the
Fantastical and apocalyptic end of our tumultuous
    decade of courtship.
My only regret is how I signed my name
But that will never matter.
Because baby

you are my Earth
So when I finally get out of this bed
My cold feet will find their place on you
And when I die, the greatest fate I can think of for
    my old body
Is for you to take it and use every part you need to
    keep going
Just keep going
I will always do more for you than I will ever realize
And you will always do more for me than I will ever
    realize
And even if I never came back.
I'd die knowing I'd still have been your prize.
Baby, gravity keeps me bound to you.

Because I allow it to.

All this to say that I am sated.
I understand.
It takes so much to hold my hand while
I wade through sand
But I have you at my back.
And you on my skin
And you holding me up

I don't know if I'll ever go to sleep now that all of
    you have managed
To get me out of bed.
How could I?
I am surrounded.
I am the impossible blue sky.

❧ 14 ❧

I KNOW. I WILL. I DO

by Emmalia Petra Fae George
and
Marissa Alexa McCool
"Ris n' Priss"

LET'S DO IT, GIRL

My head is blank

Let's write to each other then, being totally honest. Let's make your diary a poem/conversation. I'll keep giving cues, though, and we can go as emotionally deep as necessary.

I'm already in one because I'm awaiting you. Or is that the start? Okay, put a title or something so we can keep notes up here.

Say it, Priss. Say it as fucking raw as you feel.

꧁

DIARY ENTRY

I don't want you to fall into a hole at work.

What hole could be worse than being without you?

I don't know about worse, but it is still this cosmic void thing.

Like the nihilism under the layers of aesthetic in a noir movie.

Except it can't be reasoned with, because it knows you better than you expect and it doesn't make sense—well, any sense that you're familiar with.

It doesn't have to make sense

My love, none of this would make sense to most

But we are not most

We are us

So you leave.

Right? I'm terrified. I'm trying so hard to trust you and me as

well. It's hard to let go. But I want it, and want you I
need you.

Yes, and wanting something so much is terrifying

We've been taught through experience

And have the scars to show

That what we want, what we need

Gets taken away

And we feel that pain, unwanted though it is

Merely through the potential of its occurrence

Alas. My Priss, I know this well

For I felt it too, and have those moments too

But there isn't a second of regret

In anything that involves loving you

No matter other, no looking back

I never knew this feeling would come in twos.

When you spend your whole life having to explain

Not having to feels invalid

But there's a difference between caution and validity.

Is there though? They're at least correlated

We learn from our past, and it sticks with us

Sometimes even when we learn differently

Some days I don't feel like I've ever learned anything,

If you hadn't, you would have no worry

This wouldn't be an issue at all

That's why they say ignorance is bliss

Unless you ride that line where you're just smart enough to be the dumbest person in the room.

Yet, my love, you are not dumb

You've been told you are

And some part of you believes it

No one ever said I was stupid. They just went about their lives as if I was—that telling me would only make it worse somehow.

Communication is as much action as it is verbal

But people who aren't autistic don't realize that.

No, they do not, and yet here we are

Fearing similarly, feeling similarly

Terrified both that the rug will be pulled out

But knowing in our selves

That we wouldn't do it to the other

And I know you won't.

And I know you won't.

So what happens now?

The crossroads of our pursuit, the emotional charge

We live for what we think is as real as it is

We love hard, we fall hard

And it took us over 30 years

To know this fall

It's less like falling, and more like windsurfing. We have parachutes.

(every time you italicize my words I feel personally attacked

for some reason)

I know, it's coming from a good place, and it's fine. My brain is irrational.

Love is irrational, go with it

But it's not—it's our brain saying "hey this person is immensely attractive, let's flood out all the endorphins forever"

Irrational doesn't mean it's wrong or unnatural

It means that despite everything

We've found and chosen each other

Even in writing together where I italicize

Just so my brain knows the difference

But when it bothers you,

I stop

Your feelings are more important

Because I love you

And you

Are

Valid

I know. But that feels like... I hear "you are valid" tossed around my Facebook feed so frequently it feels like it means nothing. And you mean everything. And so those words can't be good enough.

I do.

I do.

The words aren't good enough

Not on their own

The love I feel for you

Is beyond those words

Beyond this life

But it doesn't make them less true

And I do not say

What I do not mean

I believe you. And you know that.

I believe you. And that's why I'm here

Arguing with your brain

Despite it all

Despite it how?

Despite how much we both know it hurts

To not be believed

Even subconsciously

And how much it hurts

To have our hearts and trust broken

We believe

Not just because we want to

But because this is so good

That we have to convince ourselves

All over again

Even though

We already know

Is that how this works, though? Are we going to spend forever

*convincing ourselves? I'm okay with that, but there has to be
more to it. We are more than that.*

I never want to write the word "I" again. We are we.

What's wrong with convincing ourselves

That's what never stop courting means

Reassurance and effort and passion

Do not die with time

*I understand. I want to run away. With you. From
everything.*

We can always run away

Together

That's what we do

Simply by looking into each other's eyes

The world ceases to be

When I'm alone

And there in the moment

With you

Does it ever. It's needles on my skin.

And you're the breath in my lungs

I'll re-convince you every goddamn day

Whether you need me to

Or not

Don't ever stop.

I won't.

I'm exhausted. My meds make me get sleepy much easier.

Then sleep, babydoll. I'll be here

When you rise again

But I don't want to. I want to go to sleep with Carla when she comes instead of staying up late.

I know, my love

I promise, I'm not going anywhere

Because you're coming here

This time

Okay. I love you.

I love you

Two days.

Closer to one

What do you think?

I think I'm sleepy, but it's perfect. I want to write more of it later. Unless you think it's done.

I feel like we could write a second entry, or a second verse or a part two

No reason to end it all there even though it's a perfect conclusion to that section

Okay. I'm going to lay down for a few. This felt really good. I love you.

I love you. Sleep, my Queen. I'll still be here.

☙

PART TWO

I was so embarrassed

The most humiliating thing

That's ever happened to me

How in the world did you still love me

After I thought the world had ended?

I'm here now.

I love you.

The world didn't end, darling

It just shifted

You were tired, scared, worried, nervous, amazing, beautiful, brilliant, considerate, graceful

And then you weren't for a few minutes.

And that's okay.

Despite how much we try

We're still beholden to our bodies.

We are fallible

And so is everyone

No one else heard the tree fall, and it doesn't matter

You're safe.

I love you.

I'm here now.

I wanted to be so beautiful

I wanted to be the girl that screamed

And stood proud

And spoke with dignity

I wore something pretty

I wanted you to be proud

Because I was convinced that you'd lose interest

I don't know how you even saw me

I am in constant awe of you

And all in that one moment

That catharsis

Turned into the unleashing, the purge

Of all that worry and fear

Because I'd already fallen

So

Fucking

Hard

Well.

I don't know why you strive to be beautiful

You can't climb a plateau. You're already there.

You really think I'd get bored of someone who's spent her whole life insisting to be heard?

I was right there and bright as the sun

When I pushed you fell.

I felt your body relent.

You are here because you chose it.

You changed how I define myself

Vulnerability can't go farther than that

Now I can't imagine

Ever being defined

Without you

Within the confines of our lexicon

We strive to strip away cryptic layers.

We've taken a bomb to the site

We are the foundation still remaining

When everything else has vaporized

We'll remain fused under nuclear sunrise.

I'm always so scared

That people will run away

When they find how many layers

There actually are

Just like I ran away

From who I truly was

My entire life

Because I was afraid

Of proving everyone else right

You may have ran, but you found your destination

And fuck if you don't revel in it

Radiantly

...I want to make you a grand feast of sorts

Touch your taste buds with notes so sweet and melodic

Let me feed you.

You bring out feelings in me

I didn't realize were in the realm

Of possibility

I knew it the moment you pushed me

Kissed me

Loved me

Touched me

And now, two days away

I'm craving it like lifeblood

Needing it like breathing

Don't let me starve

I can't do this without you anymore

And I don't want to

You won't ever have to

Never again

The hands are slow slugs

But we are salted moonshine

Drifting down the airwaves.

Do you need me like I need you?

Absolutely yes.

No question.

Do you dream of me like I dream of you?

Yes. Even when awake.

Would you have fallen in love with me

Before we transitioned?

Yes. That's why I don't mind seeing you before

It wasn't all of you, but it is part of your history

I love it.

Have we always been gay and just afraid of admitting it? Or did we just realize it with each other?

I don't think it matters.

Will you love me when I get surgery? When I'm laid up and my Little self for a week? When I need help to stand and can't lift anything? When I can't make love to you the way I can now?

You will be happier with your body, and more comfortable in every aspect of your life

Remember how it felt to take hormones the first time?

It's gonna be even better

Your heart will shine

And we will all surround you

You are safe and loved no less, my child.

What about me? Will you love me?

I do. I will. Always.

I am. You are.

Always.

I think we're done!

But wait, my love

It isn't just me

There is another, the more vulnerable one

She needs to hear it too,

Don't you think?

Yes.

The sweetest of little ones.

Two friends at her side

Ever restless and scared

Ever 11

Ever warm and worried

You are safe

You are loved

You are here

And so are we

We three

Stand watch over you

Guardians of the violet one

We three

Found our place

And it is in your service.

Never worry and close your eyes

Your heart is held.

Oh, how it is ever held.

✿ 15 ✿

BOY MEETS GIRL

by Marissa Alexa McCool

IT TOOK ME 13 YEARS TO COME OUT.

13 years before I came out is when I got the name Marissa. That was three years after my girl friends in high school put makeup on me for the first time. Then a second time. Then every day, until a guy named Jesse called me a fag and beat me up in the bathroom. I stopped doing it then.

That was two years after my late friend Lindsay asked me to wear her clothes and took a picture. I pretended it was funny. Secretly, it made me feel alive in a way that I hadn't known I felt vacant. Not in an adrenaline rush kind of way, but in the "I'm actually a person who exists" kind of way.

Vacant is how I lived, slowly introducing my "other half" named Marissa to all my girlfriends. The few who knew would check with me if they were cool with Marissa, and wouldn't let me get serious if she wasn't. I had good friends.

But it wasn't enough.

When I yelled in Pastor Carl's face, some people think the "fuck you" was at him. They're wrong. Within those words were years of fear that led me to suppress who I was.

Fear of losing every single person I loved, knew, and would ever meet. Fear of never seeing my kids again. Fear of never being worthy of love. Fear of never "passing" enough. Fear that my family would disown me.

Fear that I would be alone.

I lived for most of my life as a vacant shell that other people called a name and a pronoun that chipped away at what was left of my heart. Every "he" that should've been a "she," every "handsome" that should've been a "pretty," every suit that should've been a dress, every time my mother asked me what was wrong. Even when I admitted that I had been raped, I could not bring myself to tell her I was really her daughter. Deep inside, I didn't think she'd ever believe me.

Outside of the people who already knew, my husband watched as every single night, I'd cry myself to sleep, hating what I saw in the mirror and wanting to thaw the numbness that buried everything I ever wanted. He dried every tear for years before most people knew who I was.

When I came out, everything I ever wanted in life came true, but you also have to understand the anxiety that came along with the decision to live authentically. I spent so much time in so many places. Each person I told, every time I spoke up to correct someone, the letters and messages I sent, the conversations I had, I had to anticipate the worst in case it happened.

Most times, it didn't.

Then I see some centerlord lamenting free speech or special snowflakes because we have the audacity to not put up with your mistakes like you got a hobby wrong, because it's a mild inconvenience to them and it's much easier to write everyone off than consider someone else's agency.

I see that, and compare it with every anxiety I attack I had before I told every person in my life; including some who no longer are.

For anything I've lost, by facing that anxiety, I've gained more than I could ever have hoped to know. I have thousands of affirming, loving, and supporting people in my life, and it's because I went through every one of those anxiety attacks and told everyone the truth, eventually.

And I keep telling those stories so that one day, a young trans kid can tell everyone they know, and hopefully they can react as nonchalantly as my own children did: with a shrug and asking why we didn't tell them sooner.

It was worth it. It was always worth it. I'd rather be a sensitive, triggered tr*nny snowflake than ever exist vacant and unauthentic ever again.

❧ 16 ❧

DEVYN

by Marissa Alexa McCool

I'VE WRITTEN A LOT ABOUT MY HUSBAND, AIDEN. HE'S even in this book, and two of the others. My book *Passing Cars* has an entire chapter about how we met, and *The PC Lie* featured the story of our unique wedding.

I've written a lot about Emmalia, most of it in this book. I met her as I was in the process of putting these pieces together, and by the time the deadline was getting close, we were writing her diary entries together on Google Docs, as well as appearing in *The Friendly Atheist* and on *Embrace the Void* together. I also had her on both my podcasts within a short amount of time, including dedicating an entire episode to just how gay we are for each other.

Devyn deserves their own chapter, and it's only been recently that I've been able to articulate just how much they mean to me. It's not that I've wanted to leave them out of previous pieces, it's only that meeting

Emmalia sparked something between Devyn and I that had always been there, but it became gasoline on a match.

Emmalia has her music and podcasting. Aiden has his podcasting. Devyn has a story that they speak so casually about, but it still blows my mind every time.

They were raised in a Pentecostal cult and have experiences that I can say I've heard and understand all I want, but I will never be able to truly empathize with what that must've been like.

Never being able to cut their hair, not being allowed to partake in anything cultural, being married off young in order to keep someone in the church... All of these things happened to a person, and they got out of it. They had to escape their own life. Many more never do, and this still goes on to this day.

They escaped, got really into the BDSM and music scenes, traveled the world as a dominatrix, and ended up in Seattle, where they suffered serious health issues that led them to being hospitalized for a long period of time.

Nobody came to visit. No one.

When they decided they needed to get out and live again, the second thing they did was go to a live show of *God Awful Movies* in Seattle. I knew they were a non-binary person who followed the show, had just gotten their name changed the same day I'd meet them, and that I'd see them there.

Also, they were androgynous as fuck and it was endearing to me. Who would've guessed that androgyny was my particular flavor, right?

I was there with what they called "an entourage"— Aiden, my ex-girlfriend (not at the time), and my adopted mother Karen Garst. I'd been drinking wine at a purple bar all day, then on the way there, kissed my ex in front of a hate pastor, so I was on cloud nine as it was.

I walked into the loft bar where the VIP pre-show was being held, and I instantly noticed their eyes on me. I pretended to not notice because, despite what certain events in my life may indicate, I'm a rather shy person about approaching people I've never met, even if I know I'm meeting them there.

They were out of the hospital recently and still needed their walker to move around. I suppose a bit of me went into caretaker mode, but most of me was becoming enveloped in who this person was. They had an aura, and sonnets could be written about their eyes. They were looking at me in a way that I didn't recognize, one which remains unique to this day.

I still have a hard time believing when they tell me what that look is. I'll explain later.

I made sure they could lean on me when having to get up and down stairs, and that Eli sat them next to me in the theater... because I'm so subtle. I even let them hold Trans Pride Monster throughout the show and tried to pretend I wasn't ridiculously attracted to them.

They were out of spoons by the end and couldn't go to the after party, which served as a way to flirt with them over Facebook any time the show was mentioned. I'd say "wow, that after party was amazing, I can't believe what you did there." Things like that. Again, I've never been subtle in my life.

The flirting continued. For those who aren't aware, I'm very submissive, even for a trans girl. I know, everyone believes that not just all trans girls, but trans people in general, are submissives. Devyn was not. Devyn was a domme in a way that I'd never experienced, and we were soon discussing me returning to Seattle for a weekend for, shall we say, an experience.

Most of my life, I'd been shamed for how I felt and what I wanted sexually. If I wasn't shamed for it, I was reminded about how I was never going to find it, how only other submissives would ever be with me, and how I was looking for a unicorn that didn't exist.

Yes, that had me intrigued, but who this person was when we weren't talking kink also did. They were incredibly empathetic, gracious, generous with their time, expressive, romantic, and eloquent. I could easily get swept up in their words, whether it was about music, poetry, the sky—it didn't matter. The fact that they also had interest in me with kink was a bonus.

When I arrived in Seattle that weekend about a month after we'd met there for GAM, I was toast the minute I saw them in the airport. They'd gone all-out in giving me a good time, and later, I'd find out this was because they thought I would be a summer fling because I traveled so much and probably met up with people like this all the time.

We stayed at a bourgeois hotel with door people and framed black-and-white pictures of men who killed for sport on the wall, and that room became a paradise of gayness. I'll spare you the details, but let's just say they had me under hypnosis.

It wasn't the royal treatment or what went on behind closed doors that got me addicted to them, though. It was walking down Pike Place and never running out of things to say. It was walking along the ocean and finding beauty externally and in each other's stories. It was when the Blue Angels flew over the city, and they left their walker and grabbed me by the ears, gently pushed me to a quieter area, and talked me down until the loud noises went away. From that point on, we called noises "Blue Angels" when they'd get too loud for me.

I took care of them in helping them get up stairs, they took care of me in managing symptoms of my autism. It was innate.

The pain in our eyes and hearts when I had to fly back home was so great, they immediately knew they never wanted to feel it again. Being that far apart after a connection that rare, deep, and exciting was never going to do. Fortunately, they weren't tied to the area too much and worked for a company that had plenty of places to work in the Twin Cities, and within another month, they were sharing a home with me.

It was awkward at first, and definitely a transition for them. Going from living by themselves to a family with two kids was not what living the kink lifestyle was like, but we bonded in other ways, like sharing books, podcasts, rides to work, Saturday morning pancakes, and affection most of all. They were a tactile, affectionate person in the way that I always desperately needed, and I could get lost in it for hours. In a reverse of many typical relationships, our companionate love grew before our passionate love did.

Then, when Emmalia came along and collared me, at first they seemed devastated that they couldn't be what I needed. This was never the case. Devyn had bonded with Aiden and the kids and become family. There was no question that they were staying with us and going wherever we went. It was a unit, even if we decided to stop being poly, which I almost did until I met Emmalia. The frame of mind was "no longer poly, except Devyn."

The spark of Emmalia entering our lives made a lot of the love (and kink) rise to the surface. They had told me something many times that never sank in until then: "You are my world, baby girl." It took a relationship shakeup to realize they truly meant it. They weren't interested in being famous or visible, or even dating anyone else, as they've been exclusive to me since we began. Their life was me.

It's a lot to accept by someone with abandonment and family issues, who has always felt like the outsider at family gatherings and in her own relationships even (before Aiden).

But they meant it, and our passion came alive in ways that left that weekend in Seattle in the dust. We became inseparable. I began sitting in their lap every day before work, and we couldn't stop being affectionate with each other. We shared a bed more often, and they shared me with Emmalia in a way that everyone consented to and loved so much.

Devyn knows me inside and out—my tics, mannerisms, needs, weaknesses, and desires. They already know and are prepared for anything that happens. But I can't tell you enough what that look in their eyes truly means to me when I see it. They look at me like I am their world, because I am. I even feel arrogant saying that, because we've been taught that someone who treats you that way probably has ulterior motives, but not Devyn.

We've built our own little world with each other, and our family all has what they do to help. Devyn snuggles my daughter and cheers Aiden up when he's sad and teaches Emmalia about me and talks about music and games with Michael. But they get tackle hugs from me. Gentle ones, as their illness makes it difficult, as does any time we travel or become intimate. It doesn't come without cost, and it breaks my heart into a million pieces when I hear them in pain, crying, throwing up, and suffering.

Every single second I spend with them is precious in a

way I've never known. Emmalia has Jenny, Aiden gets lost in his own head and has his own needs and desires to be in love with men, plus the home life makes a lot of balancing required.

But Devyn and I just *are*. I love them so deeply, so intimately, and every touch we share has its own universe of light and magic that I wish I could articulate better. I feel beyond unworthy for someone to treat me so amazing, even though as they read this, they're shaking their head and saying, "Stop that." Their laugh is intoxicating and arousing when the circumstances are right. The world is in their eyes, and whenever we share that glance or that deep stare, I am one with the cosmic energy between us.

So, if you've been reading my work and wondering why the stories of Aiden and Emmalia are so prevalent, but Devyn just seems to be there, rest assured that is not the case. That's the way Devyn lives; going to work, coming home, and being with me. And it's one of the best occurrences of my entire life, and every second is a privilege.

I have a feeling they may be proposing to me soon. Even though I'm already legally married, I still want to be a bride someday, and fuck the state anyway. They mentioned a ring being on the way. We've talked about it. It's going to happen, and though a "commitment ceremony" it may be in the eyes of those who see it as a legal arrangement, it's going to be a wedding. We'll be celebrating committing our lives to each other, even though the state says we can only do that with one person.

I don't care. They don't care. We've been in love since that exciting and strange night in Seattle, and we've never looked back and never will. Devyn Lennex, I love you so much, and when Lennex gets added to my name, I will beam with pride when anyone says it the same way as when people connect it with Aiden's. I'm so grateful that the weird little world of podcasting somehow got us together, because I have no idea how I ever lived without you. I never want to again.

And we're kinky as fuck. They're my Sai. Deal with it.

❧ 17 ❧

THE OTHER WAR

by Renee James

BACK IN 1970, I WAS A YOUNG MALE SOLDIER SERVING in Vietnam. I was a base camp troop, so unlike soldiers in the field whose enemies were death and terror, my enemies were boredom and monotony.

Which is why I signed on when a friend of mine came to me with an illicit scheme for sneaking off to Bangkok for a few days of partying in the sex capital of Asia.

This wasn't a smart decision. We would be absent without leave—AWOL, if you will—in a war zone, which in the prickly military code of justice is considered desertion. If we got caught, we could kiss the rest of our lives goodbye.

But boredom is a powerful motivator.

So for three days and nights, my friend and I frolicked in the bars, cavorted with prostitutes, and drank and ate like kings.

On the fourth day, I woke up with a young woman I

didn't recognize, the tell-tale symptoms of gonorrhea which I did recognize, and the shocking news from my friend that he couldn't figure out how to get a ride back to Vietnam.

The other thing was I was broke. I called home to get money wired to me—then tried to figure out where I'd sleep and eat until the money arrived.

Which is how I fell into the care of the young woman who spent the night with me. She called herself Suzy Wong, after the title character in a sixties movie about an Asian prostitute. She took me to a medical clinic operated by the U.S. military. There was a door for women and another one for men, and when you got inside, there were different colors of tape on the floor leading to different procedures.

I followed the color for venereal disease. 20 minutes later, I emerged with a sore butt. Not a word had been spoken.

Suzy Wong took me home. She lived in a tidy, comfortable flat in a pleasant neighborhood. She introduced me to her roommate, another young woman, very pretty and the mother of a toddler. I didn't know much about such things back then, but I could tell they were lovers. Nothing overt, just the way they looked at each other.

Plus, even then, I could see how sex with men had to be dehumanizing for Suzy Wong—a different stranger every night, many of us unpleasant.

We spent the afternoon together. First, me watching Suzy transform herself from the sultry sex goddess I'd met in the bar to a pretty young woman with a nice smile. There was a lot of hair to un-pin and some of it came off. There were false eyelashes big enough to squash mosquitoes. And there was padding and a lot of makeup.

Guys aren't supposed to be interested in such things,

but I was rapt. For years, I had been fighting to suppress a growing desire somewhere deep inside myself to be a girl. I sometimes had dangerous dreams of having a sex change and wearing beautiful dresses like Suzy did, and having beautiful hair done up like Suzy's, and being admired for my beauty and grace.

I always erased these images as fast as I could. I didn't understand them, but I knew they were dangerous.

Suzy Wong sensed I was different. At one point, she asked if I'd like to have a man for the night. I blushed and said no.

In the morning, Suzy asked if I'd like to go to the beauty salon with her. She smiled when she said it. She had read me. Of course I went.

The beauty salon was as transportive for me as the prostitute bars were for my fellow soldiers. I watched Suzy get made up. I watched them do her nails and makeup and hair, making her look like a Hollywood actress.

As I watched, I imagined it was me they were working on—a me who was 5'5" and pretty with perky, round breasts and full lips and delicate hands.

I hid these thoughts from everyone, and I even tried to hide them from myself, though as the years went on, it became impossible to deny them.

In the end, my money came from home. I got my hotel room back, and Suzy stayed with me that last night. We got a ride back to the war zone the next day. I laid a huge tip on Suzy Wong, more than she'd make in many months and she was happy for it, though she proposed marriage to me yet again, as she had many times in our days together.

I pointed out that she didn't really enjoy intimacy with men. She denied it, but just enough to save face. The thing was, she would have traded anything for a future where she was safe and comfortable and could live in dignity. She wanted to escape from a place where her only career options were sewing in a sweatshop for a dollar a day or selling her body to strangers.

I've thought about her thousands of times over the years, especially as I began to accept who I was. I always wish I'd given her more money. I always wish that what I did give her helped her escape the prison she was in.

And when I start feeling sorry for myself for having such a large, unwomanly body, I think, what if I had the choice? I could be what I am—a woman in a man's body, but with a nice family and a good career—or I could be Suzy Wong, a beautiful young prostitute investing her youth in the lusts of men with no names and facing a future of poverty and broken dreams.

I always accept my own reality, but I always hope we can change the realities for people like Suzy Wong, and for my transgender brothers and sisters.

18

GIVE ME STALLS IN THE MEN'S RESTROOM OR GIVE ME DEATH

by Logan Reiss

I don't want to get rid of my vagina.
As a transgender man, I was told I should,
But I don't want to.
People talk about gatekeeping
And making sure everyone feels included
But I'm being kept out by the people
Saying I'm valid.
When the people who say you shouldn't ask
What people have in their pants
Start asking what you *want* in your pants,
We have a problem.

My boyfriend wanted a penis, so he bought one.
I saved the money for gummy bears
And was told I wasn't thinking straight.
And what a loaded sentence that is,

To assume I've ever thought "straight."
I don't want sex,
I don't want a penis,
And I don't want you asking about it.
It's becoming tiresome for people
To ask when I want bottom surgery
When I'm quite happy with the bottom I've got.
It's not that I want my vagina;
It's that I don't want anything else.
Sure, get rid of my uterus
And give it to a woman who needs it,
But leave the rest alone.
If it's trans solidarity for me
To rip these lumps off my chest
And give them to someone else,
Then it should be trans solidarity
Not to ask me
What I'd like to have
In my pants;
No matter your insinuations and meanings,
The answer is nothing.

So before my voice drops
And my chest gets flat,
I'd like some peace and quiet
About my unmentionables.

19

DON'T TELL ME

by Hadar Rubin

Don't tell me.

Don't tell me I'm this when I'm not. Don't try to make me bow down to the narrow margins you choose for yourselves.

Don't tell me what to do or how, just don't tell me. Don't tell me I'm actually captive, because I will say it back to your face—regarding love, compassion, thinking.

Don't tell me, because I'll say it back.

Put yourselves in someone else's shoes before you speak. Have your head and heart in place of theirs, and then maybe you could really talk to each other. But until the day we have empathy machines, for the very least open your eyes and ears and *listen* to the person you're talking to.

Up until the moment you've opened your mouths and criticized my choices, you did not hear a word from me about your own choices. Have I judged you, to your face, about the choices you've made in your love life? Your diet? Your life? Have I ever told you that maybe you shouldn't have a child, eat a steak, or love only one person until you die?

If you didn't ask me, if the topic didn't come up naturally, the answer is probably no, it didn't happen. It doesn't mean I don't want to promote issues I care about; of course I do. I don't hide my opinions on almost any topic. But I'm not "telling you."

Until now.

Now I am telling you. I'm telling you, of course you can love more than one. Did you stop loving your parents when you started dating? Did you lose your love of your firstborn when your second came along?

Of course you can be committed to more than one person. Do you only care about the feelings of that one friend and not the other's? Did you stop having friends when you got married?

Of course you can be "like that," even if you're single. What do my tendencies have to do with my status?

And I will also tell you that no, you don't have to embark on this journey or lifestyle only from a stable relationship that was first monogamous. No, you don't have to come back home every single night to sleep with "the one."

You could! Of course you could.

But you don't have to.

I'm telling you, of course you can give up on animal-based products. Of course. You can also raise healthy and happy cats and dogs. No, you don't have to live in want—no B-12 or iron deficiencies, without missing out on burgers or ice cream or compassion. Because (almost) anything has a solution. There's plenty of food choices.

I'm telling you, yes, there are women who don't want to

have children. Yes, you can get to your 30s and not hear the biological clock ticking. Or maybe it is ticking, but other things matter more, and you don't have to have babies if you don't want to.

I'm telling you, yes, you can choose. You can choose your way of choosing.

You can change your mind.

You can change your position, you opinion, your attitude toward something. You're allowed to regret, rethink, change. To walk away. To come back.

Don't try to tell me I can't because you can't. Don't tell me that I can't because, here I am. Don't try to erase me just because you don't understand me, and do not try to discredit my stance as being the result of ignorance or need.

I did walk away, and came back, tried, considered, got hurt, reconsidered. I've learned, checked, tasted, regretted, decided, and walked a very long and winding road into myself and back out again. I've never been more complete, and every piece of my identity was subject for a serious conversation with myself.

Before you have these conversations with yourselves, don't dare try to tell me who I am.

20

PULSE: A REFLECTION

WRITTEN JUNE 14TH, 2016

by Marissa Alexa McCool

IF YOU DON'T ALREADY HAVE THIS EXPERIENCE, I WANT you to imagine that from a young age, or even recently, you began to realize you were different from most of the people around you.

Maybe you forced yourself to pretend you liked certain things to fit in. Maybe you wore certain things that didn't reflect who you were, but you thought it was the only option. Maybe you convinced yourself you were crazy because the other people associating with you seemed to identify so simply, or just talk about their opposite gender in a way that didn't make sense to you, but it was all you knew.

As you grew up, or learned more about yourself, the dissociation was only exacerbated. It didn't pass like so many "phases" older people would use to excuse your behavior rather than validate who you were. The feelings increased, the distance between you and others did as well, and you were left without words to explain what was happening, but just knew something was different.

Not wrong, but different; that's important to distinguish.

Then one day, you realized there were others like you —an entire community waiting to embrace you. There were also other communities who told you that you were sinful just for existing, that you would burn in hell for eternity because the god who loves everyone made an exception for you, and that you weren't who you thought you were.

You could be converted, changed, pray it away. You didn't have the right to be who you felt, and these people felt they could take away your right to identify yourself because they didn't understand or agree with it.

As you face these constant attacks, these bullying, online messages, name-calling, physical abuse, verbal abuse, and everything in between, those who remain consistent and back up what they say about loving people and their friends grow closer to you, because they don't feel you're holding back anymore. They see the difference, that there's not this resistance or repression that was obvious before, but unable to be articulated.

The conflict of greater love against greater hatred seemed to delete the middle and draw you to one of two extremes. Both were challenging to deal with at times for different reasons, but you still couldn't explain what it was.

Then one day, however it happened, you learned that there were words for what you were. Whether you happened upon them online, from a friend, or god forbid, through Tumblr (ZOMGZ EVERYONE RUINS EVERYTHING LOL), a word speaks to you from the screen, a word that makes you sit up straight and say, "Yes! That's it!

That's what I am! That's what I've been feeling all this time!"

It doesn't change anything, except to give you a name. A label doesn't change what you are or how you feel, but it does give some sense of permanent and concrete identity. No longer do you have to question what it is or wonder if there's just something wrong with you, it's that. That word right there, in one instant, solidifies confusion and gives you something shorthand to explain who you are.

How do some people respond to this?

"It's so hard to keep up. Why do we need labels? They didn't have these when I was a kid. Are you sure that's what you are? Isn't this just a phase? How do you know you're this if you're not that?

"You'll get through this when you find the right person. You don't really want to identify as a different gender or no gender at all. You're not asexual, you've just not met the right person. You're not gay, you're just confused. You're not bi, you just can't choose. Pan isn't even a thing, quit making things up.

"So many special snowflakes who think they're special. Where does it end? How can you not be the gender on your birth certificate? How can you want to be in love with more person than one? Why don't you want to get married? Why don't you want to have children?

"Why don't you believe in God? You need to pray. I'll pray for you, rather than validate who you are."

And when someone attacks who you are, however they do it, you stand up for yourself because you're sick of this bullshit. What's the response then?

"God, everyone's so PC these days. People are offended by everything. It was just a joke, relax.

"It's okay, I'm a feminist, but... It's okay, I'm an ally, but...

"I don't mind gay people; just don't hit on me. It's okay, I can say 'fag' because my friend's brother's cousin is gay, so that makes it okay.

"I didn't mean 'tranny' like a joke; it's just a word, get over it.

"This is why I'm voting for Trump, he says what's on his mind and calls out the PC bullshit."

Surprisingly, people start feeling victimized because others are claiming their own identities and not going along with who they pray to. They have rights now and aren't backing down. They become convinced that it's Christians who are the real victims. Their beliefs are being persecuted because they aren't the only ones who have a voice anymore, and that prevents them from expressing their religion somehow.

Not to mention it tears at the fabric of the country and its values, because we don't all pray to the same invisible sky daddy, so that of course means that the world will end because of it.

A presidential candidate comes along who tells them that they're the true victims and the good people, and if we just got rid of everything that protected ethnic and social minorities, everything would be absolutely awesome again.

"It's not you," he says. "It's them."

When hate is validated, false persecution complexes are acknowledged, and people are encouraged to take matters into their own hands, violence follows. There's murder. There's rape. There's bathroom bills that are passed. People refuse to serve others for not agreeing with their "lifestyle."

And there's a phrase that validates all this bullshit. "Sincerely-held religious beliefs."

Whether it's passing bathroom bills, refusing service at a restaurant, calling you a whore for daring to wear that skirt or want access to birth control, or throwing rocks at an inter-racial couple, it's somehow all okay because of "sincerely-held religious beliefs."

Then it reaches a breaking point, a climax—someone takes an assault rifle and murders 50 people. Maybe you knew some of them, maybe you didn't, but being a part of that community that embraced you, it hits you harder than any other attack would have. People like you were the ones singled out, and unlike the other attacks where it was against a solitary person or disassociated through bigoted legislature, this was a direct attack on not just the people there, but everyone who is a part of that community.

Then you reflect on when other tragic events like this have taken place. We all became one people for a few hours at least, and hope that this might be the time that people drop their bigoted, hateful shit and come together to support a community in pain.

For a good portion of people, this did happen, and it's sad that it has to be a political statement to be a decent human being under these or any other circumstances.

But what do others do?

Make jokes. Laugh at PC "libtards" who won't know which group to defend. Tell them they deserved it. Celebrate murder of their own fellow citizens. Somehow consider them all pedophiles and say they deserve to be murdered.

The people who consider the WBC a hate group say pretty much the same things the WBC does, and don't see the correlation because they don't picket funerals.

And of course there will always be the conspiracy theorists, because somehow everything that happens is a secret act by the government that they also claim is useless and can't do anything right.

Oh, and many of those same people screamed #All-LivesMatter when others were claiming their right to be equal citizens. Funny how they don't seem to matter to them in this instance. For once, someone was claiming their right to exist and to be equal, and it wasn't including them, so they had to force themselves into it.

"Don't forget about me, I'm also important. My life matters too!" they wailed, while failing to acknowledge that the "only" did not exist in front of the slogan. For once, it wasn't about them, and they couldn't handle that.

And I say if you're going to consider yourself pro-life and yet celebrate the murder of people, you need a new word. If you call yourself a patriot and yet claim that a mass murder of your own countrypeople was a benevolent act of God, you're a selective patriot, at best. If you call yourself an ally, but remain silent when the community is attacked, you just not yelling "fag!" at people or comparing trans people to monkeys isn't enough. You need to speak up.

And if you're going to say that God loves everyone and all lives matter, at least be honest about your asterisk. "God loves everyone*, except for people I don't agree with politically, socially, religiously, sexually, or philosophically."

And "All lives matter*, except for ethnic and social minorities, non-binary people, non-cis people, non-straight people, non-Christian people, non-whatever-I-am-people, because when I say all lives matter, what I really mean is my life matters, and I don't want you to forget about me."

Complacency is dangerous, and many felt the fight for the community was over when marriage equality became the law of the land. Many, including myself, remarked that the fight shifted to attacking trans people because they'd lost the fight on gay rights, so they needed another minority to attack.

What happened in Orlando was an attack on who many of us are. It was an attack on the community that openly embraced us and let us know that we weren't alone in this world just because we weren't like most of the people around us. If you can't understand that, I don't know how make it more clear and concise to you. Our very way of life was assaulted, and 50 people lost their lives.

Why? Because some guy saw two guys kissing and decided that everyone like that had to die.

So, let's make that perfectly clear: Two people of presumably the same gender kissed, which led to some asshole committing mass murder.

And yet it's our community who is tearing the entire country apart. That makes sense.

Do not be silent. Do not let this pass. Do not allow people to make jokes at the expense of this. Do not celebrate murder or validate the hatred and ignorance of others.

And please, those who were scared, do not hide who you are because this might happen to you. Not being true to yourself is scarier than any risk you face once you've opened up. As an atheist, all I can believe in is the one life I know that I have, and I don't want to see anyone waste theirs because they're afraid that some nutcase might get trigger-happy for someone daring to be who they are.

This is unacceptable, and this needs to be addressed for what it is: a hate crime, mass murder, an attack on our ways of life, and proof that the fight was not over when marriage equality passed.

The fight for equality has gained a few victories, but the election of someone like Donald Trump only demonstrates just how easily time and rights can be rolled back. If you don't believe me, just remember that the Emancipation Proclamation was issued in 1863, and it only took nine years to completely wipe out all the progress made in at least half the country. Rights were gained, and then taken away. Few people lived long enough to see when they would be restored.

We can't let that happen again. If God loves everyone and all lives matter, start acting like it.

#WeAreOrlando

21

BLUNT

by Mela Blust

LOOKING FOR GOD

ran away one summer
turned some dusty corner, looking for god
and his greasy hands made their way to my zipper.
passed me around the hotel room like a cheap bottle
    of wine,
hard hands holding my gasping mouth
to the cheap comforter.
forcing me to breathe in the sins
of a thousand other lonely souls
who passed by this little intersection
looking for god.

ROMANCE

hard fingers where the pale meets the pink
dirty mouth hunger dripping drink
savor sweet sanguine soaking hole
suck me honey i wont tell a soul
hammer hard pavement meets the dirt
tell me why the boys they always hurt

WOMAN

am I polite enough?
am I right enough?
I can be pretty
not too pretty
products on my skin
I still can't let you in
walk this way, no not that way
don't wear that skirt
ouch please that hurts
and no one understands why
I'm so tired.

#METOO

remember when I stood before you like
a brand new coin?
How sad to tarnish my shine for
the benefit of your loins.

22

QUEER LATINX

by Princess Harmony

THIS DECEMBER MARKS AN IMPORTANT ACHIEVEMENT in my transition! After 17 years of waiting, I'll be undergoing my orchiectomy.

This surgery, the first and potentially only genital surgery I'll have, is something I've wanted since I was a scrawny little brown boy. In honor of something this big, I've been reflecting on my experiences in my childhood and teenage years. Specifically, I've been reflecting on what it means to have been a queer and trans person in a Latinx family.

Growing up in a Latin household, simply being sexually attracted to men (something that I've known since kindergarten) was not something that was even entertained as a thought, let alone being a boy who know she's really a girl. Latinx culture strongly emphasizes masculinity and heterosexuality as being the most important qualities that a person assigned male at birth should have.

This often comes in the form of toxic masculinity and abuse for people who don't appear to comply with this picture of manhood. This strangles the life out of trans women and queer boys, emotionally, psychologically, and sometimes literally.

In my family, there was such a strong emphasis on heterosexuality and masculinity. Uncles and cousins emphasized and tried to drill into my head their macho ideas of manhood. I had to act like a boy, but being around mostly women—in their eyes—had made me soft. So what they did was send me to be with men in my family to toughen me up and make me a man.

Needless to say, they didn't make a man out of me, and I wasn't comfortable or happy with these attempts to make me one at all.

I had to perform masculinity for them because the idea of me being feminine, enjoying feminine things, and rejecting masculinity were so unconscionable that they weren't options for me. The emphasis that was placed on me to look (sexually) at women, even as a child, was symbolic of how unconscionable it was to be any sort of queer.

I'd known by kindergarten that I was sexually attracted to men. Simply to look at a man made my heart flutter and my body tingle, but I could never describe these feelings to anyone.

My sexuality and gender as a child were things I ended up having to explore independently of my family, because I could never have gone to them to talk about my feelings. Even if I were a heterosexual boy, I'm unsure I could have talked about my sexuality to my family. Sexuality simply is not something spoken about in Latinx families, to the harm of our youth. Since queer subjects were never covered in school and I had nobody in my family that I could turn to, I turned to whatever I could find.

Had my family, had Latinx families in general, been more open to talking about sexuality, I might have avoided the potholes and pitfalls that I had hit, the predators I attracted. I might have had a childhood where I could be myself and a young adulthood where I didn't have to turn to sex work. But since I lacked that, my sexuality as a queer youth was a place of emotional landmines that is still impossible to parse.

At nine years old, most people think sex and gender are the last things on children's minds, but it was always on mine. I started having sex with older boys and adult men at that age, and they were the ones who taught me what my parents and what school did not. They taught me about my body and how I would end up having queer sex.

My sexuality was something that I learned of and embraced early, I had sexual relationships with boys and men much of the time that I was growing up with nobody to really help me navigate it. I was the object of predation when I thought I was the object of love. Had I a family that I could have gone to as a queer child, this would have been avoided.

When I was 11, I relied on public access television, weekly circulars from New York City, and Jerry Springer to teach me the words for my identity. When I'd visit New York, public access channels would play escort ads at night, and that was how I first saw a woman with the kind of body I wanted.

Weekly newspapers were the same. I learned that I was a "shemale," a "transsexual." Although I rarely had access to it, the *Village Voice* showed me the kind of woman I was going to grow up to be. It was how I learned that escorting (sex work) was what women like me did. It was how it became an option when I eventually transitioned.

That was what life was for me. I grew up with access or experiences that were too much for a child to comprehend. Yet coming out and getting guidance was not an option.

For some queer and trans youth, coming out as a child or teen can mean eventual acceptance and very few roadblocks. For others, especially queer and trans youth of color, it means rejection, abuse, and eventual disownment. This is why 65% of all homeless queer and trans youth are youth of color.

Even if one isn't disowned, the environment can be hostile and suffocating, which leads to poor mental health outcomes for those who grow up in households that are anti-queer. Additionally, the lack of queer-friendly sexual education in households ultimately contributes to the high level of queer people of color who acquire sexually transmitted infections and HIV. The household that queer youth of color grow up in, even after one has acquired their own personal independence, heavily impacts the behaviors of queer people of color.

To handle dysphoria and the inability to even speak of my queerness to anyone related to me, I turned to drugs to dull the pain. For years, I used and abused drugs and alcohol until I ultimately needed the aid of inpatient and outpatient rehabs and 12-step groups.

It wasn't until my cousins took me to get an HIV test when I was 19 that I actually considered HIV as a risk to my health, despite having sexually active for a decade. This is not unique to me, and unfortunately cannot be combatted until communities of color address queerphobia.

I call on communities of color, especially during the holiday season when so many queer youth of color can't be with their blood families, to examine the queerphobia and toxic masculinity that our cultures embrace or force onto children. What can we each individually do to make our families and cultural spaces safer for queer youth, especially trans girls?

We can de-stress the importance of hypermasculinity in our cultures. By showing that hypermasculinity isn't a prerequisite for being a respected person, queer youth who don't wish to be masculine can see that they will still be loved and wanted if they choose to reject masculinity. It would also lead to more respect for women and feminine people, which would have a positive impact on youth whether they were queer or not.

Straight, cisgender people who are friendly to queer people need to do their part in fighting the anti-queer attitudes in their families. Queer people—all queer people—need allies who are willing to fight for us even when we aren't around. By challenging the anti-queer mindsets of people in the family, you eventually change cultural spaces by encouraging people to do better for queer folks.

Everyone should encourage open and frank discussions about sex and sexuality that are inclusive of queer sex and the shape that can take. Instead of relying on schools to teach sexual education—which they barely do, even for heterosexual people—we should do more to have those conversations to educate our youth.

I ended up on relying upon people who very well could have been preying on me to show me what sex was. Nobody should have to risk that in order to learn.

There's so much cultural work across all demographics which needs to be done to create a society that accepts and respects queer and trans people. But we can start on even the smallest level to create that society. We have to do it to prevent any more queer youth homelessness.

My parents and family, faced with the very real possibility of losing me, eventually accepted me, for the most part. Though I have cousins and aunts concerned with whether or not I'll turn their children queer or trans, and I have no wish to ever engage with them again—I survived. I feel that it's my duty to use my experience to create a better world for queer and trans youth. That's what all of us who survived and grew up have to do.

❧ 23 ❧

GRAY SPACE

by Aiden Xavier McCool

HERE I AM, STANDING IN FRONT OF YOU, FLESH AND bone, realistic to the touch. I am, and I am not. I am tangible, and I am pure fiction. I am made of contradictions. How can I be both at once? As impossible—or cliché—as it sounds, it's happening right now.

People are uncomfortable challenging their perception of what is normal; something as trivial as skin color goes too far for some. In recent years, society has come far in beginning to accept the fact that "not all women have vaginas," boosting the acceptance and visibility of trans women. Yet the fact that not all men have a penis is never brought up, ignoring that trans men and non-binary individuals exist.

Trans men are as numerous, and present, as trans women, but are drastically underrepresented in comparison. Speculation is made as to why. Grief and anger over such an injustice is made, and then is mostly forgotten. No one really looks into why we are less visible, aside from our ability to blend in with our cisgender counterparts, but I can see numerous reasons why that is.

Our culture is still overwhelmingly biased in favor of men, and yet we put far too much of an emphasis, too much value, on being male. Men are under great pressure to keep up a certain façade, a certain attitude: always aloof and somewhat emotionally detached; enjoys some forms of sport; attracted to women, or other men, and always thinking about sex; always tough; always confident; always masculine.

Anything less than or different from these traits discounts from a man's perceived identity. Nothing distances a man from these age-old traits like having a vagina.

Trans men are under even more pressure to emulate these traits and be accepted as a man. Some trans men choose to blend in for their safety or their personal preference; some will never tell their friends or loved ones that they are transgender.

Trans men have the unique ability to give birth, another idea that is quite far removed from the male traits listed. An act that is usually celebrated as a miracle is ignored, or venomously ridiculed, by many people, their perception being that you have the ability to give birth and you get pregnant, you are a woman and were only pretending to be a man, or for lack of a better generalization, you're a freak.

Not many consider all of the planning that had gone into this, the fact that his partner might not be able to give birth, or that it would be unsafe for their partner to do so; or simply because it was his choice to do so. He and his partner are mocked and invalidated because he did something that was traditionally done by women only.

The mainstream media is not necessarily kind to us, either. During a speaking engagement that Marissa did over the summer, she asked the audience to name a trans male activist that was not Buck Angel, and the audience was silent.

There are some foreign films about trans men, or have characters who are trans men, but not many that have been made or distributed in the United States. The only one that got a lot of media attention, *Boys Don't Cry*, starred Hillary Swank, a cisgender woman.

I can forgive that it was far more difficult for many trans men and women to be visible at the time the movie was filmed, but things have changed in 18 years; and yet there has not been a surge in trans male actors or movies starring trans male characters.

We are not often accepted by cis men because we do not have a penis or were not born with one, and therefore, we are not "real" men. At the same time, we are accepted by cis women a little more openly than cis men, but there are still some areas of discrimination and discomfort because of our gender identity, or through some bigotry expressed by some women.

I was reminded of this during the performance of *The Vagina Monologues* that Marissa was part of this past February. The writer/director of the show is notoriously against any changes to her show-and has been known to revoke the license to put on the performance-if anything has been altered. After 20 years, the show progressed a bit by acknowledging that "not all women have a vagina," but stopped short of acknowledging trans men or non-binary individuals by barely giving a nod to "those who have vaginas."

People see me, they know who I am, and they know I

exist. At the same time, I am a non-person, a myth from a fairy tale. I am not a man because I still have a vagina, I'm faking it because I have the ability to give birth, and I must not have hated being a girl that much if I decided to get pregnant. I'm not a woman because I don't identify as one, I am sometimes seen as a threat; and I am simply one of "those who have a vagina."

The path ahead of me is blocked by gatekeepers, and I cannot go back, and so I exist in the unexplored, clouded, gray space between the gender binary; waiting for the gates ahead of me to open even just a crack.

I am waiting for the mist to clear, waiting for the world to see and acknowledge us as more than just freaks, or vague entities that the term "transgender" loosely applies to.

❧ 24 ❧

POLY CRACKERS

by Hadar Rubin

WHO GETS INTO YOUR VAGINA, IF YOU HAVE ONE? How do you choose? Is it the looks, the smell, the particular organ? Hands, tongue, lips, maybe a toy? Maybe you don't want anyone or anything there at all.

Maybe you don't have a vagina. That's okay. Not everybody has to, and actually, sometimes, like once a month, it kinda looks like a slaughterhouse. Sometimes I wish I could skip.

Some people can't choose for themselves. Some people choose for themselves, but then regret it and cannot—or will not—correct the mistake. Some horrible, horrible people force themselves on others.

My heart goes out to anyone who can't or couldn't choose for themselves. Not just about this specific issue, but about anything. I wish you lives full of choices—good choices.

But how *do* you choose? I mean, personally, as long as no one is getting hurt, I don't actually care—I might be curious, but it's my own problem, not yours. But I am constantly being told that my choices and my decisions about my own vagina (and heart, but leave that for another day) are weird, or wrong, or crazy, or deluded. And worse things too.

And let's not get into what God probably has to say about me. We're trying to have a nice conversation.

I know how I choose, and the way to my vagina goes through my brain, and usually through my heart too. But my interest and my emotions aren't restricted to one person only, and that's what I'm talking about today.

How do you choose, why do you choose, why did I choose to not limit myself to just one partner, for the rest of our lives, amen?

Just as if we're talking about ice cream flavors, sexual positions, a band or a musician, or a field of study, or having more than one child...

The bottom line for me is, I think that my vagina would rather have in her multiple people I love and respect, instead of just one that a non-existent god chose for us.

25

STREAMLINED

by Dharma Kelleher

MRS. CAMP, MY FIRST GRADE TEACHER, RELEASED US for recess. It was my first day of school in the year 1972 in what was then the small town of Snellville, Georgia. The sun was bright. The sky was sapphire blue. But something was very, very wrong.

Mrs. Camp sent the girls down the hill to jump rope and play house. The boys hustled up the hill to play kickball. I instinctively headed down the hill to join the other girls.

Until Mrs. Camp intervened.

"No," she said, grabbing hold of my shoulders. "You need to go up the hill with the other boys."

That was when I knew the gods or the Fates or the Universe or Cthulhu had made a major mistake. I was a girl. How could no one see that I was a girl? I felt like a girl. I thought like a girl. Girls made sense to me. Boys were alien beings from another world who liked to push people around.

But what was I to do? So I shut up and did as I was told, knowing to the core of my being there had been a huge mix-up.

I learned to keep my truth secret. My survival depended on absolute secrecy, even if I didn't understand what my truth was. The Deep South in the 1970s wasn't exactly a bastion of inclusivity and progressive thinking.

A few years later, I learned that boy bodies and girl bodies were different. And for some reason, I'd been born with a dangly, ugly piece of flesh hanging down where a vagina should have been. It was a mistake. I was a mistake, an ugly duckling. But I had no way to become beautiful, streamlined swan.

Somehow, others knew there was something not right about me. From grade school on, I was the target of every bully in school. They called me wimp. Sissy. Faggot. Queer. Pansy. That last one was a frequent taunt from my mother.

In silence, I yearned and ached to be myself. I discovered that I could push that dangly piece of flesh up into my body and pretend that I had the right parts. Just to be streamlined. To look like I was supposed to look, if only for a minute.

I had no name for what I was. The word "transgender" didn't exist, and the word "transsexual" was never used in polite comedy.

There was no internet at that time. No Google. No Facebook. No Wikipedia. I had no context for what I was; I only knew that I was a freak. A mistake. A pervert. A sissy. For daring to believe the impossible. That despite the dangly piece of flesh between my legs, I was a girl.

Sure, Christine Jorgensen and Renee Richards were

occasionally mentioned as punchlines in sitcoms. Those freaks. Those abominations. I thought, *I can't be like them. Please God, don't let me be that.* And yet somehow, I knew that was what I was.

I was a freak. I was an abomination.

When puberty began, testosterone was like fuel to the fire of my dysphoria. My desire to live as a woman, to have a woman's body, to be a woman became excruciating.

I struggled to hide it. Not just hide. I viciously fought against it. I was sure that if only worked hard enough, believed enough, and prayed enough, if I just pretended to be man enough, the desire to be a woman would go away.

But I couldn't stop myself from cross-dressing in secret. No matter how much I prayed. No matter how much I drank. No matter how much I fought against this insanity, I couldn't escape it. Because it was me. And I couldn't escape me.

And then I heard about a supermodel who had once been a man: Tula, otherwise known as Caroline Cossey. And get this, she dared to pose nude in *Penthouse*.

This revelation shook my world. I went to the local convenience store and bought the issue. It was the only time I ever bought a men's magazine.

I looked at the photos. I read the all-too-brief article. And I knew. I knew who I was. And I knew I wasn't alone. And I knew what I had to do.

For months, I searched everywhere I could imagine for people like me. I looked in the local alternative weekly and the gay newspaper. Nothing. I checked the gay bookstores, the library, everywhere.

Then finally, I found a listing in the White Pages phone directory, a single line that read: *Transsexual support group.*

I called that number. I joined that group. And I began a new adventure to somehow get rid of that nasty piece of flesh between my legs and reshape it into a vagina. My vagina. Because despite my efforts at crossdressing early on, it was never about the clothes. It was never about the makeup. I spend my days in T-shirts and jeans. It wasn't Christie Brinkley that I longed to be; it was Joan Jett. Bold, butch, brash, badass. And every bit a woman.

Yes, it hurt that my then-wife divorced me. It hurt when my mother called me an abomination and told me I'd be an ugly woman. It hurt when all of my friends abandoned me. It hurt when my employer fired me. It hurt when church after church kicked me out.

But that was nothing compared to realizing the hope, the dream of becoming the woman I was meant to be.

For five years, I stumbled my way through a series of bad jobs, some of them illegal. I managed to change my name and get started on estrogen. Slowly, my body began to change. I was taken under the wing of a group of drag queens, whom I call my fairy drag mothers. They taught me how to speak and walk and dress and put on makeup.

Along the way, I met a man who later turned out to be an abusive rage-aholic, a perfect match to my codependent self, desperate to be loved, desperate for approval, desperate to be seen as a woman. Both of us, as it turned out, were also alcoholics. So naturally, we got married.

Even as I was becoming a woman on the outside, on the inside, I was dying. My husband became more and more abusive until one night, he headed off to the bars and I decided to end my pain by swallowing 60 aspirin and chasing them down with a half-bottle of whiskey.

I was tired of being abused and berated and gaslighted. I

was tired of being told I was worthless and stupid and insensitive by a man I was desperate to make love me.

Good news—I didn't die that night. But I made a decision to stop drinking. I joined AA. I eventually left him, three separate times because being the codependent that I was, I kept going back, hoping this time he would love me.

Eventually, I got a restraining order against him and left him for good. I flew up to Portland, Oregon and I lay on that surgeon's table. I spread out my arms as they hooked up the IV to put me to sleep. And I took a leap. A joyous leap into the future I longed for.

Recovery was painful, at first. Then it was merely uncomfortable to sit for long period of time. My thanks to whoever invented the foam rubber donut.

One of my most vivid memories was meeting my vagina for the first time. As it happened, it was on February 14th. Valentine's Day. V-Day. My new birthday.

The doctor came in and removed the packing. Like a clown pulling a multicolored streamer from their mouth, the surgeon pulled out this endless length of gauze from my newly created vagina. It was the strangest sensation, overwhelming with emotions, joy and gratitude and relief, but also sadness for all that I had endured to reach that moment.

When I started to cry, the surgeon looked at me strangely and asked, "What's wrong?"

"Nothing. I don't know. Just a lot of feelings."

He handed me a mirror and I saw my vagina for the first time. Shaved. Angry. Swollen. A little deformed. Like a newborn baby.

A month later, after doing my morning dilation, I was kneeling on the bed, facing the mirror over my dresser. I was naked, and there was no ugly piece of flesh dangling between my legs. My body was beautifully streamlined the way it was meant to be. And I felt this rush of joy words alone will never describe.

I've spent half of my 52 years living as my true self. My streamlined self. And I have no regrets.

26

PLANET: OCCUPIED

by Marissa Alexa McCool

I remember the first time I took estradiol
The neurons in my brain
That had been dormant for so long
Finally connected their wires inside my head
Triggering new emotions that were so raw
But as real as they'd ever been,
Not bereft to the incorrect chemical
Blasting its way through my body
Like an occupying hostile force
That conversely needs you
To survive

That feeling
That struggle
That invasion
How did you ever manage to live without it

Except you know
You know the truth
It's impossible to know the poison
When you've grown immune
It only becomes poison again
When you return
To what was
Once familiar
And now
Feels as foreign
As the new chemical
Should never
Have had to

Can that happen too with new love?

How preposterous to think
How can you
The one they call a rock star
And have a bunch of cute nicknames for
The one who has been downloaded
Hundreds of thousands of times
Read, listened to, heard, respected
Graduated, married, partnered, validated
How can you possibly
Have had anything
Missing?

She checks the boxes
She knows your heart so well
It's like she designed it herself
Her eyes stare through you
Knowing full well that she owns them

And everything else
Because love isn't a pie
And love from a woman
Doesn't take away
From the man you love
Or the inseparable, maudlin enby
Who watch out for you
Like a security team on high alert

She's there
She's driven there before
Because she knows the routes
The shortcuts, the side roads,
The timing of the lights
She maximizes time, energy,
Everything she needs
To arrive at the front door of your heart
With the floor plan
Imprinted in her mind
She takes the damaged goods
And replaces them with better ones
She takes out the light
And makes the new ones shine brighter
She gives you a purple aura
Somehow more alive
Than the one
You thought was already perfect
She's now inside

How can you feel like this?
How can you consider her different?
How can you consider trans women different?
Trans women are as much women

As cis women
But she's different
They're different
But her especially
She makes you feel alive
In ways that only can be understood
By recognizing the lack of existence
In the vacancy that lay wasted
In broken dreams, hearts
And grievous acceptance

You're allowed to be truly gay, Marissa
You're allowed to love a trans woman
Like you never could a cis woman
Remember Ashley
Remember how hard she made you cry
You never cried like that when a cis woman
Broke your heart
This was different
This cut deeper than you knew
You had the capacity for
And now she's there, Ris
Now the one
Who loves you
As much as you
Love her
She's
Right
There

The journeys that were written off
With love, but explained away
Don't worry, she'll be back

This is just what she does
She wants to come with you
Walk beside you
Wander with you
Explore the unexplored
And partake in your passion
She loves your alter
Treats her as well as you
Never questioned for a second
She writes words
And speaks them
In such a manner
That leave you a mere puddle
Trembling with emotions
That despite your wordsmith reputation
You can't describe for the life of you

Oh, Leonard!
Leonard!
Help me articulate this!
You've only helped me with suicides before
Can this be real?
Can this be believed?
Can a woman who made you accept your sexuality
And who loves you
Really be this omnipresent?
She spoke poetry in motion
She throttled your defenses like butter
And she stayed
And she wants to
And you're not left
Explaining away
The way you think or how you feel

Or the fact that you give consent
Even with how many times it's been taken
Without permission

Let her take you, Ris
She means what she says
No words like those could be faked
Fall
You're safe here
Fall
You're loved here
Fall
She's the one you've been waiting for
Look at her, she's there
Right there waiting
Like you've been desperate to feel
Since you heard that song
With your first girlfriend
In high school

Those girls
And all the others
They weren't like her
No one's like her
It's not even a fair comparison
She leaves them all in the dust
She stole your heart
She occupies your mind
And she's comfortable
Where so many others
Have had to run away
When they've gotten too deep
I like it here, she says

I want to stay
You are hers
She is yours
Let it be

My gothic songbird
My vampire queen
My transy-pansy
Fuck, I'm so gay for her
Your parents were right, weren't they?
You love the same gender
They just got the gender wrong
But they were right
You are so
Fucking
Gay

Accept this
Acknowledge it
You're a gay trans woman
Married to a gay trans man
In love with an enby
But this is who you are
It's okay
Nothing changes these loves
Or hers in kindness
But what you share
That planet you've built
To escape
When no one else understands
She's already there
Building the foundation
Together

With you
You don't have to explain how you got there
Anymore
She's all in
She's there
We can't share it all the time
But we can some of the time
Enough of the time
And that's enough
She's enough
You're enough
Accept it, Marissa Alexa McCool
You're gay
And you've found the only one
Who could've ever
Made you realize that
Because she's the one
Who was meant to

You're right
I hope she stays
Inevitable

27

DEPRIVATION OF DENIAL

by Marissa Alexa McCool

Whisper in the wind to the long-lost souls of time's
  erosion
Twist with the question mark of wonder upon tepid
  reveal
Shiver with anticipating regret and salience
Leave no skeleton behind.

Crest within the depths of sentience
Drift upon the invisible cemetery of invented cures
  of the memory's virus
Dance upon conquering the expectation of
  permanent regression
Sense the impending sequential upheaval and place
  the cornerstone on the ring
Circle upon the beaming evenflow in the
  deprivation of denial

Exposed within secure confines of intimate solitude

Dot the horizon of the altered timeline
where passive settling embraced the victory
over the jaws of questioning
The void remains a long shot in the dark horse
running ever-increasingly toward a finish line
that remains obviously impregnable
upon the altered ridge of oblivion
You cannot go back to what you once convinced
    yourself out of to stay alive
You're alive now
That was only the breaking dawn of the aria of
    certainty

Clutch the tendrils of undue erasure and the
    suppressing instincts
to accept the expectations of the bridled masses
She who stands upon the ridge with blanket
    consent
and the collared's lock
straightens the previously uncorrected societal
    scoliosis
Let the breeze carry of the robe what the subject
    cannot
Become the solitary monarch of the willingly
    conquered
Rise with the crescent moon and deliver the life
    sentence
Transcribe the Others once unmentionable
Release the captor
Execute the hypnosis
Accept yours with hers and tear up the out clause

No returns
No exchanges
No refunds

Borders and layers lay discarded in the frozen pool
decaying upon obsolescence of strivance
toward rounding up and the inflation of fractions
Complete the equation
No check
Impress upon the clean copy with the dissertation
    of blissful serenity
Say the words
Unretracted
Undeniable
Unquestionable
One

No simplification

❧ 28 ❧

TRAVEL

by Marissa Alexa McCool

AN INCOMPLETE LIST OF QUESTIONS WHILE DRIVING:

Is someone following me?
How is that sticker telling me I'm lesser to them?
How far am I from the nearest city?
Is anyone else using this rest stop?
Does this rest stop have a family restroom?
How many cars with conservative bumper stickers
    are at this rest stop?
Is anyone looking at me walking in?
What if I have to stop for gas?
Is that person looking at me strangely?
Is anyone else around?
Is this place well-lit?
Will you go with me?
Why do I have to see the cashier?

Is it even worth stopping?
Is it dark enough to stop on the side of the road?
What if someone sees me?
What if someone listened to <insert awful
    conservative argument here>?
What if they clock me?
What if I get pulled over?
Why do I have to ask for a key?
Why don't they have a self-checkout?
Should I call AAA?
Should I correct the person who stopped to help?
Should I pretend that "sir" didn't hurt?
Should I just use this McDonald's cup?
Why do I have to ask these things?

AN INCOMPLETE LIST OF QUESTIONS WHILE FLYING:

Should I try to stealth it?
What kind of look will I get when I show my ID?
How did they "sir" me after seeing it?
Should I wear no makeup and dissociate?
Should I be myself and brace for the inevitable?
Do I know they're gonna stop me again?
Do I tell the agent I already know what they're
    going to ask?
Do I tell them it happens every time?
Can I stop myself from crying when their hands
    slide up my leg?
Can I stop myself from crying when their hands
    invade my groin?
Can I stop myself from crying?

Does this airport have gender-neutral restrooms?
Will the gate agent question my ticket?
Will the flight attendant misgender me too?
Will the person next to me be reading
    far-right news?
Can the guy in front of me lean back any farther?
Do I really have to go through this again to
    come home?

by Kellie Ramdeen

IT'S MY SENIOR YEAR HERE AT PENN, AND I COULD NOT be more ready to graduate and leave this place forever. While many of my peers are already starting to reminisce about their time here and are happily making the most of senior year, I'm dealing with my PTSD diagnosis and going to therapy twice a week. This year has been stressful, but unlike the rest of my time at Penn, I'm actually getting support and treatment.

My freshman year, I was raped by a guy I had considered to be one of my closest friends at Penn. I met him during NSO, and he lived in my dorm and quickly became part of my friend group and my Penn family. He would tease me and hug me and tousle my hair and make sure I got home safely after a night of partying.

One time, a group of us went out and a guy got too aggressive, and he got me away from him and made sure I was okay. He was a good friend and someone I trusted. I would go to his room to hang out with him and his roommates. I was happy and naïve and trusting.

And then, one night, he raped me.

I remember that night so vividly. I remember jokingly reminding him about his girlfriend and laughing and saying no. I remember realizing that this was not a joke and that he was actually forcing himself on me. I remember him taking off articles of my clothing and me quickly grabbing them and attempting to use them to shield myself.

I remember trying to push him off of me. I remember saying his name and crying and begging him to stop. I remember sobbing and shouting no.

And I remember eventually giving up. I remember lying there passively as he did whatever he wanted to me. I remember my head repeatedly hitting the headboard and I remember looking into his eyes and seeing nothing.

That night changed me. Everyone says that your rape doesn't define you, and while I know that's true, I'm a different person because of that night.

I don't trust people. I have anxiety. I'm depressed. I'm scared of intimacy. It's been years since that night, and I still have PTSD.

And it's fucking frustrating. I want to be over it. I want to be enjoying my senior year, and I want to be focusing on my thesis and job hunt without having this horrible trauma lingering in the background.

Since my rape, I've had other bad and sometimes scary sexual encounters. I wish people discussed the different forms healing processes can take. Because of that night, it's hard for me to set boundaries, and it's hard for me to say no. I'm always scared that people will ignore my wishes and keep going, and I would rather just go with it than be violated and ignored again.

It's degrading and dehumanizing to say no and then have it blatantly ignored. I don't want to go through that again. I don't know if I could handle it.

The summer after my freshman year, I studied abroad in London. My first weekend there, my cab driver took me to an abandoned park instead of to my dorm and sexually assaulted me. I ended up pressing charges, mostly because I found out he had done this to a few other women and the police had been looking for him.

Even though the assault was caught on CCTV, and even though a few of us accused this man of assault, the case lasted my entire sophomore year. I came back to Penn, and on top of dealing with schoolwork and extracurriculars and my trauma, I also came home to emails and phone calls from London about my case.

Sophomore year was rough. In the spring, I became overwhelmed and asked for an extension on a paper. I told my professor about my case, and he was nice and gave me the extension. That was that.

A few months later, I won my case. I feel extremely fortunate to have won, but I am still disappointed with the sentence. Because I was unable to go back to London and testify, the man was deported from England and put on a sex offenders list.

Junior year, I was a fucking mess—depressed, suicidal, skipping classes, not finishing papers on time. I eventually told a professor about my situation, and he was actually helpful. Unlike my pre–major advisor and other professors, he reached out to Special Services and got me in touch with Paige (who is my literal hero). He also checked in with me and talked to me in person.

Thank you Dr. Nishino, for being the only Penn professor to give a shit about my wellbeing, and for introducing me to resources that could have helped me so much throughout my case.

I had no idea Special Services could have helped me navigate my case. I had no idea I could go to Penn Violence Prevention for advice. I had no idea advisors are supposed to direct students to resources.

Flash forward to senior year. I'm still learning about different resources available to me. I'm finally in touch with Jess Mertz, who is a badass and an angel. I'm in touch with Malik Washington, who cares more about students' wellbeing than anyone else I've met here at Penn. Sanjana from the Women's Center has been my best advocate, and I got a CAPS referral for an incredible therapist in Center City who is helping me get me better. I feel like I finally have the tools to heal, or at least get better.

Despite this feeling of support, and despite making it to senior year and winning my case and accomplishing a lot during my time at Penn, some days are harder than others.

Sometimes I feel like I will always be that crying girl, realizing that I can't trust anybody and that people can be monsters. Sometimes I feel like death would be easier than trying to push on and keep going. Sometimes I feel like I will never be able to fully trust my friends or anyone else, and that I'll never have a successful relationship because I'll always be waiting for that person to betray me.

Sometimes I feel like I'll forever be that girl on February 21st, 2015.

❧ 30 ❧

LAST DAY OF CLASS

by Melina Rayna Svanhild Farley-Barratt

TODAY WAS MY LAST DAY IN CLASS. I UNPLUGGED MY laptop from the floor outlet in the classroom for the last time. I still have assignments to do and turn in, a final to take, and two final projects as well, but today was the last time.

It is an almost certainty that I will never be in that classroom ever again. At least as a student.

I'm crying. Let's see how many times I start that while I write this. I will never plug my laptop into that outlet again.

<*Juke Box Hero* by Foreigner is playing on my phone.>

This is major milestone in my life, one that will be among a collection of many, all part of the experience of graduating next week.

<*Urgent* by Foreigner is playing now.>

That's right, I'm graduating! It's "only" an AS in Computer Programing and Analysis, and it took me 2.5

years to do even with already having an AA for the general stuff, but I have never worked so hard at school in my life.

I'm crying again.

I made the dean's list one semester, one of my early classes I ended with a grade over 100%, and before this semester I had only one core class that was not an A these past two years. This semester has been particularly difficult, so I am only slightly disappointed in knowing I will likely get straight Bs, maybe even a C or two.

It helps knowing that it was more a factor of needing more time to do everything, or not being able to utilize as much time due to my health issues as well as parenting problems. I know the material.

<*Relax* by Frankie Goes to Hollywood is playing—why did they go with that name for their band anyway?>

It is not like graduating from high school. That's more like "finally, I'm free!" while being unleashed on the adult world. It also isn't like getting married or having a baby. Those feel more like the beginning of things, solid. Sure, there are new things for me after this, but those are far more ethereal, uncertain, vague.

<*Ooh La La* by Goldfrapp is playing—I love the retro style of the video, and the sparkly metallic horse is amazing.>

<*Goodbye Stranger* by Supertramp is playing—I had to do some stuff in the kitchen; it's important to eat every now and then.>

This is more like your last day at a job you didn't have to leave and loved doing. I did that once; I remember it well. By pure coincidence, hurricane Charlie was due to go through our area that very weekend. I spent my last few hours marking all the cords on my computer, labeling them for ease of reinstallation, because we were putting it in plastic bags to protect it from possible water damage if the wind broke the windows. That was the last time I punched a paper timecard.

<*Dare* by the Gorillaz is playing.>

I was sad to go. The end... of a part of my life. Such things also bring me around to thinking about my life, and how much of it I have left. Anyone who has followed me closely knows my life expectancy is... an open question. I started school with the idea that "in 10 years I will either be dead, dying, or doing well" on the hope I would be doing well.

<*Clint Eastwood* by the Gorillaz is playing—"my future, is coming on, is coming on, is coming on...">

Even when I said that, I wasn't sure how many years into those 10 I already was. I am certain that at the end of those 10, the question of my life expectancy will be clearer than it is now. Hell, in three years, it'll probably clearer than it is now.

<*Rhinestone Eyes* by the Gorillaz is playing—"with the paralytic dreams that we all seem to keep, drive on engines till they weep..." Anyone who knows me in person knows I like to drop quotes of songs into conversations, often I deliberately use whatever song happens to be playing around us even if it doesn't really make sense.>

Considering that, what do I do next? Where do I go from here? (This is a semi-rhetorical question; I really don't want any responses with advice on the subject. Except for those who... you know if you are one.)

<*On Melancholy Hill* by the Gorillaz is playing.>

Do I gamble more on the "doing well"? Do I spend more years of my life moving toward a BA degree? Should I go ahead and enter the workforce now? Can I enter the workforce now, considering my health issues?

I have disability now, so it would be easy enough to continue with school, at least for now. My family would be better off, at least for now, if I did enter the workforce. I'd probably start at about twice what I'm getting through disability, not counting deductions.

<*Plastic Beach* by the Gorillaz is playing.>

But what if I really only have three to five more good years, a very real possibility? Would it make sense to spend my remaining time in school or work then?

<*I'm Still Standing* from *Sing*, the soundtrack is playing —no I didn't plan this, not really. Yeah, I knew it was coming; it is my playlist, after all.>

I could spend a lot of time doing the things I love, with and/or for the people I love. I could dive into my activism, or travel with or to see my friends and family even. Doing that would cause my family to stay stuck in this cramped, tiny house, though. Entering the workforce could get us out of here in a little over a year, assuming my health supported it and continued to.

<*Bad Water* by AronChupa is playing—I hate that I love this song. The religiosity really ruins it for anyone not Christian, but the message itself is almost great. Almost because of the religiosity.>

All things I have to think about. I think I have most of the next year mapped out. Hopefully I'll have more reasons to be hopeful of a longer future then.

<*She Wants Me Dead* by Cazzette & AronChupa is playing—it's a really catchy song.>

<(*Don't Fight it*) *Feel It* (*AronChupa Edit*) by Aron-Chupa from the *La Vida Nuestra* soundtrack is playing— sometimes I have to stop and think, and play a song again.>

This is the end of a part of my life. I try not to think about the end of my life itself. It's scary.

I'm crying again.

I have a project in mind I want to do. What will be left of me in 100 years? My own ancestors of a century ago I have a few names, some stories from my grandparents. Maybe even a picture or two; they were rather rare back then. I want to take some dance classes.

<*Try Everything* by Shakira from the *Zootopia* sound-track is playing.>

I think I want to leave this on that song. It seems fitting.

Next Friday I graduate!

I'm crying again.

❧ 31 ❧

BRAVE CROW

by Brave Crow

BRAVE CROW WAS UNABLE TO SUBMIT THEIR PIECE, BUT we still wanted to acknowledge them and the work they do for the Two-Spirit community.

We thank them for their contributions.

I KEPT RIDING

by Connor Scarlett

I REMEMBER MEETING IN A CAFÉ, FOCUSING NOT SO much on the words we exchanged, but on the sliding feeling as I moved my iced coffee in circles on the slippery counter.

I remember the cool, refreshing feeling of a sweating plastic cup on a warm fall day.

I remember being nervous to audition for *The Vagina Monologues* later that afternoon. I was so excited to audition that I signed up for the first slot, the very first audition. I liked the idea that I could be the person that would push people to lean into discomfort and learn something about vaginas and feminism, especially since Penn's campus was so new to me—it felt powerful to have something dedicated to the stories of women and people with vaginas, people like me.

That's the funny thing—losing and reclaiming power went hand in hand, from the very beginning of my story.

On a warm day toward the end of September, during that time of year right before the world settles into fall, I was sexually assaulted. I choose to focus on the inoffensive details, the singed edges of the events that brought my world crashing down.

Nobody is entitled to the parts that I try not to dwell on. For me, my experiences after what happened are the most important part: the isolation that I felt and the support I got from people in my life, the relationships that changed, for better or for worse, as a result of what happened.

I remember the grimy feeling of a dusty dorm window that stuck to my fingers as I tried to clear the air out of my room, the faint smell of lavender as I tried to make it a new place.

I felt like it was my fault because I didn't have anything to compare it to. My story isn't like the one that pops into most people's heads when they hear the phrase *sexual assault*. It was a story of taking without asking, not caring to ask. It was the little voice in the back of my head saying that I wouldn't let that happen to me, that it was my fault because I invited the person into my space, because it was consensual at first.

It was a feeling of dread in the pit of my stomach afterwards, opening my window and taking a scalding shower before I could feel clean, then still not feeling clean.

I remember the first therapist I was sent to, who spent more time talking about the legal definition of rape and the man who did it than she did listening to me, the fake flowers in a still-life on the wall and the furniture that tricked me into thinking it was comfortable. She questioned my experience as much as I questioned myself, an authoritative representation of all of the worrying and self-doubt that I'd been experiencing already. Could what happened to me *really* be rape?

The little voice in the back of my head echoed that therapist, who echoed the narratives in the *#metoo* stories that were flooding the headlines as we approached winter. Was I overreacting? Wasn't it my fault if I invited him into my space, acted interested at first? If I was okay at the beginning, wasn't I asking for what I got?

In the week after it happened, I told my story over and over again. Tears made the noise machine outside an office in the Women's Center feel louder. I trembled as I sat on a chair in Student Health Services, wondering if I would have to give a full account of what happened every time I came back.

The gynecologist who took my initial report had kind hands. You could tell how disgusted she was that this happens so frequently. I remember how strange it felt for her to call me "brave," a baggy title that didn't feel like it belonged to me.

Months later, the same woman stood and spoke at a Men and Masculinities Conference, talking about how she was completely surrounded by women. How she was amazed by their strength and thankful, in a line of work where men and violence are so often in the same breath, for the men who are vulnerable. Who respect and uplift women. Tears that I hadn't felt for months jumped to my eyes.

THE PART OF THE "SURVIVOR" NARRATIVE THAT DOESN'T get told is how draining it can be to exist. It became a full-time job, trying to lift the weight off my chest, to stop my head from pounding because of the stress of existing, groping for the bottom of the gnawing pit in my stomach.

When a strange man looked at me on the way to class I felt my heart in my ears, tears burning my eyes as I tried to focus on how many cracks there were on the sidewalk in front of me, and to convince myself that I was more entitled to my body than a stranger.

I cried to friends because it felt like I didn't deserve to occupy space, even my own. I wanted to dissolve into nothing, to crawl out of my own skin. I spent nights against warm bodies in twin beds, grateful for the familiar smells of my friends, the foreign feeling of their sheets.

I remember how thankful I was for the little bright spots in the weeks after it happened. I ran into a mentor a few days after it happened and was able to explain, for the first time, as much as I wanted, without being pressured to give more details, to prove that what happened wasn't okay.

When I told my roommate, she helped me look up campus resources and change my sheets. I slept with the blanket that my grandmother made me before I went off to college and, on a particularly bad day, found a tiny, embroidered *I love you* that I hadn't noticed on one of the corners.

I sent the old sheets home with my brother. Ryan was one of the first people that I told. The weekend after it happened, he rescued me. We spent a Saturday reclaiming my space.

He brought me the well-loved stuffed Cat in the Hat that I loved so much as a child so that I wouldn't be alone at night. I ran my fingers over the tag on his back, traced his mangled whiskers, looked at the spot on his nose where love had worn away the fuzz.

Ryan and I put up the stars, Pleiades and Cygnus, Capricorn and Cassiopeia on my ceiling, little bright spots to keep me safe at night. When we ran out of tape, he walked with me to the grocery store, past frat parties and drunken hordes, to buy packing tape. On the way home, he carried the bags.

He brought a blanket and slept next to me, on top of the covers, and didn't complain when his neck hurt the next morning. Being a big sister gave me a purpose, something clear. He helped me more than I helped him at the beginning, and now he's my best friend. He still calls me every day just to talk.

I found safer spaces and ways to cope on campus. V-Day, the movement associated with *The Vagina Monologues*, gave me a space to be vulnerable and play with the concept of my identity as a victim, as a survivor.

Getting ready to perform my monologue, I started to think about how what I associate with the word *vagina* changed so much over the past year. Listening to the monologues was cathartic—the monologues portrayed it as a place of pleasure, violence, confusion, and education.

I began to think not only of the terrible experiences that I associated with the monologues I heard, but also how my vagina could be so essentially *me*. In reclaiming my body and sexuality, I made a big step in taking control of my trauma.

I can't tell you how many times I've been told that *healing is not linear*. Healing for me was gradual, a process that I'll never really finish.

Learning to live as a survivor looks different depending on the day—it's the small accomplishments that make me realize the progress I've made. Sometimes that means not crying in the middle of math class. Another time, it might be avoiding a panic attach when a male doctor asks me how many sexual partners I've had in the past year and examines my stomach, even though I'm only there because of a urinary tract infection.

Sometimes it feels like I'm thriving. Sometimes it doesn't.

I won't pretend that what happened hasn't changed me, that I wouldn't give anything for it never to have happened, but I have begun to see ways that this horrible thing forced me to grow, ways that it could make other people understand. I'm grateful for the friends that I've been able to rely on, for the communities I've found in the aftermath. Most of the time, I'm out of the really dark place I was in this fall and winter. Sometimes I'm not.

The point of this story isn't to canonize those who have experienced sexual violence—it's to put out what I wish someone had told me. Even though it feels impossible sometimes, things will start to get better. It was so gradual that I didn't notice how much stronger I'd become. I told myself so many times that what happened wasn't my fault, that it happened *to* me, that I wasn't a burden and that I deserved to take up space. I said it so many times that I started to believe it.

One day, I biked across the Schuylkill and went to the Mutter Museum. It was the most content I had been in a long time, alone with my thoughts and confident as an individual.

I took my time reading the explanations next to the bones and body parts. I rode back toward the university and kept riding until I reached neighborhoods I didn't know, people standing on corners chatting loudly on 52nd street, a church on 59th that had a yard full of the names of black victims of police brutality. I focused on the feeling of the wind on my knuckles.

I was a block away from my dorm when I saw the man who assaulted me. We made eye contact for the first time since what happened.

I kept riding.

❧ 33 ❧

HIDDEN BONES

by Caren Evans

GROWING UP IN THE SEVENTIES WITH TRANSGENDER *feelings, there was always a sense of aloneness.*

The patriarchy has always controlled and erased our transgender history. That is a tactic used to control and subjugate any population or community of people.

Trans people in Nazi Germany were considered "homosexual" and were led to the camps and gas chambers as quickly as the Jewish population. Similar treatment was given in all of Christian Europe, throughout the ages. There was transgender activity around early Jewish temples, and there has been transgender people in every culture and time period.

Most people today feel like it is some kind of new phenomenon because our "history" is so blank and biased. It seems like there are more trans people now only because there are fewer of us willing to hide in shame and fear of the patriarchy, and young people have more knowledge and role models.

This is a story I started writing after waking from an intense dream that was easily interpreted. I developed it by telling it at open-mics and present it at general audience events/shows.

﹟

ONE MORNING RECENTLY, I AWOKE FROM A nightmare. You see, when you kill someone, you may be haunted by it forever.

The killing was real, the victim was real. I alone know this reality because I hid her bones.

I woke with a terrible feeling, a burning question. How well are the bones hidden? Will anyone else ever find them? Other traces could be found, evidence such as hair, clothes, and shoes, but the bones were hidden well.

The killing took place in the seventies, and it was no accident. Weapons are not always what they seem.

It was at a time when I was too young and too conditioned by society to know if the girl even deserved to live. In my mind, this girl had to die; it was the only way I could see to go forward then.

Statute of Limitations. I scoff at the idea. What limits were given to me, and what limits have I put on myself? What is the limit of my mind and soul to keep this hidden? I can stand here confident I will not be punished by society for this deed, and yet I have felt relentlessly punished every single day of my life for it, and still carry the weight of the bones.

Why did I do it? The patriarchy condones, even expects a person to "kill off" one's transgender self, enforcing the gender binary over a person's freedom to embrace their unique spirit. With the whole of society complicit, it was all too easy to have these bones and deny them life. *Redemption, Resurrection.* Redemption can be a hard road to travel, bumpy, twisty, most of it uphill, but I have followed that road here tonight, to show you that it just might be possible.

Resurrection—what does that even mean? We all resurrect a little bit every day with new possibilities, new beginnings. So now I am breathing life back into these bones again. I take these little beige pills, the antidote for the testosterone that has poisoned her. I feed her estrogen. I apply it to my skin; I feel it in my bones... her bones.

I bring you this story tonight because the dream really freaked me out, I knew it was my truth, but more important are the questions I raise.

Who will tell future generations that it is righteous to be their authentic selves, without concern over an artificial gender binary, so that no one will feel pressure to "kill" the best parts of themselves in order to fit in? Who will teach them that freedom really is an individual choice? That it is impossible to gain freedom by limiting the freedom of others?

Many who think that they vote for freedom do not have a real concept of freedom, being chained willingly by the institutions that shaped them. The patriarchy has taken a hit. It has struck back with a Trump. Let's go to the polls and be as loud as we can and do something about it.

Thank you. Sweet dreams for all.

❧ 34 ❧

THE LONGEST NIGHT

by Melissa Frank

I WAS SEXUALLY ABUSED FOR 12 YEARS OF MY childhood.

It started when I was five years old and continued until I was 17. There were three men who abused me during the most vulnerable years of my life. Sometimes, even now, I look at that sentence and have a hard time believing it. I always thought that this was the worst thing that could ever happen to me...

Living with the trauma, the fear, and the shame have shaped my entire life; I spent years running from it. Once a year, I would have a remarkable breakdown; the only time that I would let out the pain. Usually this would result in sobbing for a couple of days, with no one able to console me. After those few days I would pack it all away, within its neat little box where I believed the effects of my abuse needed to live.

I lived 19 years with constant emotional roller coasters. During that time, I tried numerous depression medications, trying to solve the adversity that was my life.

But medications for depression are for changing the neurotransmitters in our brain that affect our emotions. My own depression wasn't just in my brain; it thrummed through my blood and hid in the deepest reaches of my soul.

I always thought that this was the worst thing that could ever happen to me...

I slowly found a voice through the years.

In my early 20s, I came out as bisexual. It was the mid-1990s, and the world was filled with the early beginnings of the internet. For those of us who were already on the margins, the internet became a source of joy and inclusion. Suddenly we could connect with people who were like us without having to out ourselves in person. We could hide behind the anonymity of the computer screen until we felt safe to come out.

But even in this new exciting world, I heard how *not* queer I was. After all, I wasn't a lesbian—I was just confused. Not being accepted into the queer culture was not worse than being abused for 12 years... so I was okay.

In my late 20s, I found a spiritual path that I connected with—paganism. It was great. I grew up in a Christian household, but once I was old enough to understand that "because the Bible tells me so" isn't really a reason, the magic of it was gone. I wasn't held down by the patriarchal standards of Christianity anymore, and I was able to explore a feminine side to spirituality that I never thought existed.

But every time I met other people who were pagan, I couldn't really connect with them. I couldn't find a coven, the long sought-after group of support that every book told me I needed to find the pinnacle of spirit. Even though I ended up practicing alone, it wasn't worse than being abused for 12 years... so I was fine.

In my early 30s, it all caught up with me. At the time, I was married to Ryan and we had two children—Michaela and Benedict. They were my life; in a lot of ways I was able to put aside my own pain because I had a family to take care of.

We were a close family. Our children were kind and generous; they loved us and one another so fiercely. But I should have known the pain would find a way through.

I had what could only be described as a total breakdown. I divorced my partner of 10 years and moved to Florida. Our children chose to stay in Minnesota because of their schooling, and I spent two years only seeing them sporadically. That was pretty bad, but again, it wasn't worse than being abused for 12 years... so I got through it.

Then I started seeing a counselor, and things really started looking for the first time in my life. I realized that I experienced PTSD, that I have triggers, and that I have a number of pretty bad coping mechanisms.

I started working on them, replacing them with healthier practices. My relationships fell into place, and Ryan and I came back together as a couple.

In 2014, at 39 years old, I decided to go to college. I found a new voice—an academic voice. Women and Gender Studies helped me find words for things I couldn't explain before. And the English department helped me craft the words into being.

For the first time, I stood up and told people that I was sexually abused.

For the first time, I stood up and defined myself as queer.

For the first time, I told people willingly that I was not Christian.

For the first time, I found something worth fighting for.

I graduated with my undergraduate in 2017, and began a graduate program that fall, and everything was great. After all, I experienced the worst so very long ago.

Nothing could stop me now.

And then something did.

On January 22nd, 2017, my son Benedict was murdered. He was 19 years old.

Ben was a thoughtful, happy, and considerate person. His friends tell me that he respected boundaries and was always there when they needed him, whether it was for a hug or to drive around in the middle of the night for Taco Bell. Ben always gave the best hugs; he would wrap his long, gangly arms around you and hold on tight.

Ben's murderer was his roommate, a member of the military, and a legal gun owner. We thought he was Ben's friend. Instead, his suicide letter talked about how he didn't want to be alive anymore because he felt like he couldn't die in a war like a real man should.

In the end, he chose to end Ben's life before taking his own. We were told it was instantaneous and that he didn't know, but I still have nightmares that he laid on the floor in agony, wondering why his friend would do such a thing to him. I worry that he lost his belief in friendship during those last moments of his life.

Ben died from a bullet in the side of his head, a bullet that made it so that we couldn't even see his body before they cremated him. They said that if I wanted to, I could sit next to him and they would uncover his hand.

A hand.

That was all they would allow me.

Ryan and I said no, because that image sounded like something that would haunt me my entire life.

When we went to clean the apartment, it was oppressive. The cleaners scraped the ceiling and the carpet was torn out; the floors were bare concrete, and there were still police markings on the walls from trajectories. And we now are realizing all the things that were thrown away because they were unclean-able.

We still haven't received a death certificate because of backup in the state office for ballistics tests.

In the aftermath of his murder, nothing is the same. Ben was my moonlight, a bright star in our lives. Grief eats at me in ways people can never imagine. Memories are like knives that shoot through my heart, when I think about the wonderful man Ben was, although he had very little time to live that adulthood we worked so hard to prepare him for.

There is a hole in my heart that will never be filled again—that's where Ben's memory resides.

Nothing prepared me for the excruciating agony of losing my child. I was the survivor of many evil deeds, but no number of them can prepare you for the next one.

I was not prepared to lose my hopes and dreams of a better life for my children and my grandchildren... grandchildren that I will no longer experience. Nothing can prepare someone for loss on so many levels.

I am writing this, as a legal gun owner, to tell you that we haven't done enough to protect the valuable lives around us—the lives of our children, of our friends, and of our neighbors—no matter who they are. Black and brown bodies are put on the line much more often than white bodies; all lives cannot matter, until black lives matter. Until Native lives matter. Until LGBTQ lives matter.

I'm writing this as a reminder that the future can be lost

in the blink of an eye. The standing theory is that with an assault rifle, the average shooter can fire 90 rounds in one minute—that's not just 90 lives lost; that's thousands of lives affected forever.

We deserve to ask companies and organizations to put aside their love of profits and stop creating items for sale that make guns even more dangerous, like bump stocks and high-capacity magazines.

We deserve the opportunity to ask gun owners to be conscientious and learn about the responsibilities of owning a firearm. Many nations who do not face the same issues as we do require extensive training for every person looking to purchase a firearm. We deserve to ask for a waiting period and a nationwide background check that *works*.

More than half of female homicide victims are killed by their intimate partner, and more than half of these murders are committed with firearms. Not every military person or police officer is a good guy, and not every person with a mental illness is a bad guy.

I thought I had experienced the worst thing I ever could when I was young, I thought it was all behind me. I thought that, surely, one person should never be made to feel such utter agony more than once in their lifetime.

But I am painfully aware that this is not the case.

People often tell me that they do not know how I move through my day—that I am brave. But some days I am barely making it through—some days I am happy if I get up out of bed and take a shower. Most days, one trauma leaks into the other, like pollutants leaking into pure clean water, they enter my bloodstream to taint everything inside of me.

My partner and I went from having a healthy sex life to an almost non-existent one, because every time my body has some kind of release, I start crying uncontrollably... and that includes each time I orgasm. It's embarrassing, and I've been avoiding intercourse for weeks because of it.

There is no happy ending to this story. I searched for a long time trying to find one, because I expect there to be one. Right now, my life is so full of sorrow and pain—there is little joy left in it.

But sometimes, I hear Ben's voice telling me, "I got you," something he often said when I would cajole him into doing housework or paying for Chipotle.

It's certainly not what I want. I want to live in whatever world my son is alive in. But it is a small reminder of the kind of man that Ben was—beautiful and caring. I could not be prouder to have called him mine.

❧ 35 ❧

SPECULUM

by Anonymous N

They shove a metal rod
inside my vagina. Turn the screw counterclockwise
and it opens, spreading my lips and my muscles
apart
as I scream. "It's done," the nurse says.
"You're a trooper."

The longest episode of *House*: the girl
poked and prodded and given treatments
that show no effects, months nearing years
of questions with no answers, the third doctor
        chuckling
as he says,
"You're my most challenging case."

My laundry list of symptoms

burns slow like blue flame:
pain sitting, pain walking, pain wearing jeans,
pain during sex, pain since my teens;
burns through my skull as a secret
kept at bars, in homes, at restaurants,
breaks relationships early, weighs down
as freight.
The girl who can't have sex
is the girl who can't find love.

Scraping parts of me
into a tube,
biopsy: *tests inconclusive,*
even for the rarest diseases;
the most likely result
incurable, progressively worsening,
increasing the risk of cancer by 33.6x:
5% chance
of malignancy.

I see a boy at the bar. He smiles.
I look away.

❧ 36 ❧

A THESIS OF PAIN

by Amber Auslander

THE BODY ASSIGNED FEMALE AT BIRTH IS A SITE OF pain. This is my thesis.

The supporting evidence is too easy to pinpoint, almost too obvious:

When I was nine years old, I had my first period at a flea market with my dad. I went to the bathroom and saw blood soaking through my underwear and dripping into the toilet. I passed out.

For the next three hours, I laid spread-legged in our station wagon and tried to not vomit.

Every month, once a month, my skin drained of all color and my legs shook so badly I could barely stand. Three days straight of cramping.

My mom told me I was being dramatic as rage and tears ripped through my body. I wanted it to stop. I demanded she help me make it stop.

I found out I was pregnant on December 21st, 2017. I had only started suspecting because my breasts hurt, were heavy—the body assigned female at birth carries weight.

I bled out my fetus alone in my room eight days later. It remains a stain on my bedroom floor. A nice way to spend a winter break. I remember going in and out of consciousness. I'm still not sure if it was from the contractions or the codeine.

Two months later, I had an IUD inserted to make sure I would never have to have this happen again. I don't know how to describe the feeling besides "reverse birth."

For the next month, I bled non-stop. A constant period. I learned to ignore the ache.

An abstract, a conclusion. Are they not nearly the same?

The body assigned female at birth is a site of rage.

I hope my anger is eviden(t/ce).

❧ 37 ❧

VULVODYNIA

by Sophia Griffth-Gorgati

In March of 2016
my vulva felt like it was on fire.

I was closing my sock drawer when it hit me
like a bee sting
it wouldn't stop

I wanted to scratch it
to scratch away the pain

I washed my hands in lavender soap
I tried to be gentle but
I guess my nails are sharp and
when I held out my hand
there was blood under my fingernails

A fire on my skin and a flood from my eyes
I later learned
This is vulvodynia.

Every day
women are told that they will be in
Pain
maybe for a few months
maybe for the rest of their lives
There is no cure.

There are things you can try—
Do you want
Antidepressants? they ask
We can try surgery

I respond that I want life without gasping in the
    produce section of Trader Joe's.

My life has changed;
Lazy mornings watching the sun slipping in turn
    into days that begin with
grimaces, squinted eyes from pain and not the light

I'm grateful for female gynecologists—their soft
    hands and understanding eyes
are what got me through this diagnosis
I'm grateful for the courage to write these words
    on paper

I want everyone to know this

because what they don't tell you is that
this disease affects 16% of women.

I am just one of 16% of women who feel
itching
stinging
throbbing
searing
burning
on their vulva
Every damn day.

And every damn day,
We still smile.

❧ 38 ❧

BEFORE I WAS MINE

by Anonymous A

BEFORE I WAS MINE, I WAS HIS.

The boy who whistled at me from his car, at a 14-year-old in an orange dress with blue shoulder straps and a low-slung neckline. The boy that made me think of the girl in the romantic comedy that shyly tucks her hair behind her ear, a ginger smile to herself as a stranger compliments her. The boy that made me think I was finally worthy of a catcall.

Worthy of a catcall?

Before I was mine, I was his.

The grown man that looked me over, a 14-year-old in a flannel and shorts that were appropriate for the weather, but not the society. The grown man whose look felt like the gross, slow lick of a particularly slobbery lion tasting its prey. The grown man that made me understand that the girl in the romantic comedy was not smiling, she was hiding her face behind a kind mask until she was far enough to sprint.

Before I was mine, I was his.

The legal adult that asked his friend to wingman for him when he saw the tipsy high school freshman, despite being two years out of high school. The legal adult that let word spread that, "She's out of it, dude" and that "She's probably easy." The legal adult that I had never met, I never ended up meeting officially, but that I heard about from my friend because I was so lucky I got the attention of an older guy.

Before I was mine, I was his.

The guy that thought the length of the black dress was somehow both too short and not short enough, and thought his hands might tailor it better than the lady that does it for a living. The guy that decided flipping the skirt over in the crowded dance floor might be—funny? Amusing? Appropriate? The guy that ditched when I reached down to flip it back, because I *did* mean it to be a dress and not a shirt.

Before I was mine, I was his.

The friend that watched me get plied with drinks past a reasonable limit and still thought it might be a fun time. The friend that I ended up saying good morning and goodbye to within minutes of each other with a massive question and a budding hangover in my head. The friend that I don't reach out to to ask if we did or didn't, because do I need the answer or should I live in the dark?

Before I was mine, I was his.

❧ 39 ❧

EXILE

by Jessica Kirschner

ALONE IN THE BACKYARD, SHE SITS CROSS-LEGGED IN the grass. She feels the warm summer sun and closes her eyes, awaiting her natural powers to rise from the earth and enter her body. She stretches her arms toward the sky, rippling her fingers.

She unfolds her legs and, pressing her hands down onto the earth, she rocks back and forth onto one hip and the other. Gaining energy, the warm hum of the earth music rises; dancing, the power of her own alchemy surfaces. Her agile body runs and leaps almost gaining air as she alights and poses like a tree, supple and firm, then sways and rocks as does a butterfly on a stem of a flower.

This is her secret space where she joins with the magic, beauty, and grace of the intersection between the natural world and the divine fairy world.

She wears ripped jeans and a T-shirt. A tattered piece

of cloth encircles her waist, a pink and purple translucent sari. A brass band encircles her arm—an ancient mandala. On her wrists are several worn, braided friendship bracelets. Her neck is adorned with a velvet choker and strands of plastic Mardi Gras beads. Barefoot, she dances sacred rituals performed for herself.

A child spies on her through a space in the fence. Her eye catches his and she smiles.

"What are you doing?" he asks. With the sound of his voice she feels a twinge of self-conscious doubt. But why? She is not doing anything wrong.

In the past, no one was permitted to see fairy ritual and celebration. In the old days of fairy lore, they would hold their gatherings late at night under the moon, hidden from human witnesses. Men witnessing fairy magic would rarely survive.

But she is unaware of this history. She is merely a child dancer celebrating herself.

She turns to the boy to reply, but by then the figure has disappeared. Slowly, she returns to her dance, leaving that uncomfortable feeling behind.

Then again she senses a presence. Kneeling near the flower bed and raising her arms toward the break in the fence, she sees several children staring.

Someone calls to her, "What are you doing?"

She is too far into the rapture to feel shame. She replies, "I am a beautiful fairy. I am a magical princess. I dance for all the beautiful animals of the Earth."

Suddenly from the audience on the fence, a child throws down a small stick. "Fairy, oh fairy, you need a magic wand to cast your magic spells".

She embraces the gesture and moves toward the branch on the ground. She rises with it, feeling its power in her hand, and with a graceful gesture she weaves her spell, blessing them.

The faces which look up at her seem to sparkle for a moment. She loves them with all her heart. She stops and poses with her arms extended, radiating pure energy and light.

Suddenly, there is an incomprehensible assault. Rapture is interrupted by pain. She feels an impact on the side of her face and sweaty hands pushing her down, a strike of surprise and utter violence which moves her from fright to utter despair, hopelessness and shame in despicable. Cruel speech spits from the mouth of the aggressor while laughter rises. Then a cacophony of applause from the ignorant audience.

The fairy initiation ceremony is destroyed. She lies on the ground and sobs, her energy depleted. She chokes and gasps for air. She has done nothing wrong.

After that day, she stops running and dancing in the garden behind the house. She stops celebrating. She freezes. She stops her fairy life, numb and cold. Abandoned and alone, she withdraws deep within herself and hides.

Outside, she avoids other children and walks in shame. Some of the kids call her names, speaking in such low whispers, she is unsure of what they are saying: *girly, sissy, fairy*.

What happened? Had she done something wrong? The energetic universe is transformed and she is consumed by darkness. A beautiful young girl is expelled from the fairy garden: self-exile.

WORTH LESS?

by Andreina Lamas Matheus

Wipe the sweat off your brow
Choose your weapons, arm yourself
Will you be the victim or victor tonight?

Survivors covered in our own blood
Branded filthy by history
Yet we're mocked for our misery

Not all the grenades will go off
The phallic empty shells
But one misstep may be your last

Trained to fight against each other
Claws and verbal tools on hand
Don't look the enemy in the eye

All of our sons are warlords
All of our nurture, fuel
We supply the front lines

Worth less than the next
Worth more than the whore
Our body our shield and weakness

Our value from the war paint
Smeared across our chests
Dictates how human we are

Nobody told us womanhood is a battle
With soldiers we don't volunteer
And a cause we don't know

The murder, the slaughter
The fight for survival
The rain is the tears of Athena

And the Parisian trophy
Means nothing to the fallen
Whose stories have become the footnote

❧ 41 ❧

TRUE TO SPIRIT

by Layha P. Spoonhunter

IN THE SOCIETY IN WHICH I GREW UP, MEN NEEDED TO be strong and play sports. Some considered anything else evil and contrary to the Bible. I learned social norms that men marry women and raise children. I felt that if I spoke of who I really was, I would not be accepted.

But this is who I am. I am a proud Native American; I recognize our traditions, our cultural way of life, and our spirituality is at the heart of who I am.

In the early years of my culture, people like me were accepted; we were elevated as spiritual and cultural beings. We played an important role in our tribes, possessing both male and female traits. I believe we should never judge someone for who they love, and I am truly proud of who I am. I hope someday I will get to love who I choose, both men and women. I am Two-Spirit.

Ever since I chose to be the person I truly am and

creator made me to be, I have found this life to be a blessing. Even though I have faced negativity for my choice to rise above gender norms, I have also found complete love and compassion from many supporters and family. The work isn't to gain recognition for myself, but to create a brighter future for indigenous youth where they won't be judged for who they love, what they choose to wear, or their gender.

This journey has led me to the White House, to other indigenous communities, and to hearing an American president say the words "Two Spirit."

❧ 42 ❧

RAJASTHANI QUILTS IN REDS
AND ORANGES

by Tanya Jain

WHEN I WAS A GIRL, MY DADIJI ALWAYS WORE AN exhausted expression and layers of shawls, as if every day of her life was the same battle, and all she knew to do was protect herself with soft, hand-woven Rajasthani quilts in reds and oranges.

My father, her son, would begin yelling at her, at my mother, at my sister, at me, at the world, and she would sit, wearing her shawls and her exhausted expression. I would run and hide below the dining table.

When my parents talk about this hiding place now, they discuss it as a humorous and nostalgic site, but it wasn't like a playground, it wasn't like a tree house, and it was a refuge.

I would crawl under the hard wooden table and feel safe in the darkness, in the loneliness. Sometimes it would smell like the day-old paneer sitting on the table, or the fresh flowers my Dadiji bought from the local farmer's market when she wasn't exhausted and covered in shawls.

I kept a few stubby pencils in a stack in my refuge, so when hours were long and the yelling seemed endless, I could draw stick figures on the bottom of the table, making up stories of happy families with happy futures.

When the only future heard vibrating through the walls of my home was anger and D-I-V-O-R-C-E (that hidden and shameful word; I didn't know what it meant fully, but I wanted it to happen—it never did), I would devise futures of love and support and peace. Peace, or even better, peace and *quiet*—that's what I always planned to wish for when blowing out the candles on my birthday.

Yelling is a strange sort of violence. When it starts, it feels like it will never end, and the women in my life have different experiences of living with it.

My roommate told me she likes to sit and dissociate. When her boyfriend yelled at her and screamed at her, she would sit and think of the clouds in the sky the day before, or count the number of Cheerios in the cereal bowl in front of her. She assured me it was the fastest way—that soon he would get tired and leave and she could go on.

My reaction was always to run. I wanted to get as far away from the destructive words being thrown at me as fast as possible. They were words wielded in hatred: "spoilt," "bitch," "stupid," and their very pronouncement was terrifying.

I would run under the table, to my room, to the bathroom, to the house next door, to the street down the block— as far as it took to get away. And when I was finally free, when I could finally breathe again, I felt the air in my lungs and I knew that I was alive, that I would survive. But I couldn't always run away, and running away didn't always mean I was free.

Being stuck in it became the worst feeling in the world. It was like being stuck in a snowstorm, seeing the white particles fly in the air outside, knowing if you tried to leave, if someone was able to get to you, your body would be carried away, swirling in the white sky, groundless, limitless.

Because safety was always temporary. Because the bathroom was the only room in the house that had a lock, and the lock broke with sufficient force and agitation, so I would sit in the bathroom on the toilet waiting until the door was shoved open, until I was carried into the storm.

My Dadiji always told me that she wasn't surprised by who her son became, by who her husband was, or who her father was before him, but that she simply found herself with a man who did the same things her father did, and I'm terrified I will too.

In high school I used to tell everyone I just wasn't attracted to Indian men, that my sophisticated and refined taste was something deeply misunderstood and mysterious. I looked for partners who were the complete opposite of my father. I looked for comedians, artists, stoners, writers, anything that would never remind me of the dominating, controlling, angry, powerful person I strove to avoid.

At night I would dream of healthy relationships with sweet and beautiful women and sensitive and caring men. I would reassure myself that I would never relive history, that I had learned from the pain of my childhood, and I would never let myself go through that pain again.

But my fear only grew when I got to college. I would meet men, find they had a beard that looked similar to my father's when he was young, and run in the opposite direction.

Because if they had a beard like my father, then they had a face like my father—a face that would contort with anger—and they had hands like my father—hands that would slap me and throw my things across the room—and they would have feet like my father—feet that made loud footsteps that I would listen to at night in my room, scared they would come in my direction.

So I avoided people and pretended it was fine, pretended that my fear wasn't taking over my life, that I had gotten over the trauma of my childhood.

But I read a book that said that people exposed to abuse in their childhood are more likely to accept it later in life from loved ones.

It felt like that fate was like a line on my palm, inevitable, literally carved into my skin. It would be something I wouldn't even notice. One day I would be in a loving, caring relationship, and the next I would find myself with a partner like my father, and I would be stuck like my mother, and my children would be scared like I was, and the cycle of abuse would live on with me.

I felt like I didn't have control, like my life was planned out for me with trauma and abuse just waiting for me along the way. I felt, and feel, like I will be my Dadiji. Like I have to be my Dadiji, because I don't have the agency *not* to be Dadiji, and that makes me grow weary.

Maybe one day I'll become so weary I'll begin to wear my Dadiji's exhausted expression and her soft, hand-woven Rajasthani quilts in reds and oranges.

PLAYING FAVORITES

by Amber Biesecker

When I was a child, my father told me with great
    enthusiasm
And at every opportunity
That I was his favorite daughter.
He would hold me in his arms,
Envelop me in stubble and aftershave,
And whisper to each strand of my hair
That there was no other he would rather have
    than me.

Then again, I was his only daughter.
And so I learned, early on,
To equate "favorite" with "only."

But now,
Years later,

And because of you—
The halo of your words that makes a devil out of
    an angel—
I don't feel that way anymore.

I wondered yesterday if I was your favorite.
You said, "Favorite what?"
And I said, "Favorite anything."
And the fact that you had to ask, well...
That should have been my first warning.

No—that should have been a stop sign,
Red and glaring like the light of a camera
About to record the crime of my asking.
Posterity made shame.

You never did answer.
Or so I thought,
Until I realized your silence was the answer.
Until I realized the difference between you and my
    father
Is that you have had options.
When I come to your home,
I'm not bothered so much by the fact this is a dinner
    party
As I am that what I bring to the table
Will always be the green bean casserole to someone
    else's ambrosia,
That I will always be plain and stringy among the
    other dishes
And exotic fare your travels have exposed you to.
My food is not a comfort to you.
It is instead a reminder that nostalgia tastes sweetest

When paired with something bland or bitter.

Something *healthy*.
Something *safe*.

But as I look around the table, I realize
The other chairs are empty,
Mine is the only one full,
I am the only body here, still trying to nourish
    yours,
And that is when it hits me.

That is when I realize that you are lonely,
That these delicacies all taste of dust
The wine is vinegar
And you like my green bean casserole because...
It's warm.
Some of those strange fruits had broken glass edges
And you say don't want to cut your mouth anymore,
But Jesus, they got to leave scars
You still smile at when you think no one is looking
And I?
I don't get to leave so much as lipstick on your
    collar.

A few years ago, I found out my father had almost
    had a son.
That in the womb with me,
There had been another child.
A possibility.
An option.
And I catch myself thinking,
As I try to learn a new recipe,

Something that doesn't get served in a glass dish,
Surely—surely—I would still have been his favorite
    daughter, but
What about his favorite child?

Today, I look at you, and I wonder if we are not both
    settling.

❧ 44 ❧

WHAT IF I'M NOT WHAT
HE NEEDS?

by Marissa Alexa McCool

ONE OF THE FIRST THINGS YOU LEARN ABOUT POLY IS dispelling the myth that you have to be everything to one person, and if they're not having some of their needs met, it's on you for not trying hard enough or not being what they need.

Satisfying some of your needs with others while remaining in love with your first partner is not a bad deal; in fact, it's encouraging. It loosens the pressure one may feel to be both companionate and passionate all the time. Exploring sexual dynamics or interests that the first partner doesn't have is like having best friends you also (maybe) fuck, right? Being poly allows people to fill in the blank spaces, and not expect all your wants, desires, needs, and quirks to be put on one person for the rest of your life.

Admittedly, it's easier to be on the side of the person who finds multiple loves first. All the benefits of New Relationship Energy while not having to worry about the consequences of it going sour in a few weeks and going back to being single? Economic advantages? Knowing right out of the gate that you not only will not be able to spend all your time with this new person, but that it's not remotely possible to do so? Talk about pressure being removed.

"I can see you on the first Sunday morning of every month!"

Cool, that's Prudence Day. The rest of the month I'll spend with Zoe. I already live with Zoe, so it's cool. She's married too, so she's not expecting me to be available all the time. Perfection.

It's a hell of a lot harder to be on the other side, especially when you have to admit to yourself that you may not be both the lifelong companion and utmost sexual desire to your first partner. I hesitate to use the term "primary," both to avoid hierarchical implications and because I'm referring to time elapsed in the relationship, not a ranking system.

Anyway, semantics aside, my husband and I have been through a great deal. You've read stories in this book of people who came out as transgender in various stages of life. You've read some of people who came out as gay, bi, queer, poly, etc. He and I have gone through all of this, both of us, multiple times.

In the four years we've been together, we've come out as trans, changed our names, admitted we're queer, and come to terms with our respective preferred kink roles. Most stories about partners coming out gay or trans to the other are from someone who experiences it once and doesn't go through it themselves, so I freely admit this is not only a unique situation, but a complicated one at the very least.

The list of men I find attractive is quite short. If your name isn't Chris Kluwe, it's pretty much a lost cause. But I was already in love with Aiden when he came out, and even though I've never been with another man and didn't seek relationships with other men, how I felt about him didn't change. My relationship remained passionate with him, even in periods of difficulty. Even when he was dating other men. Even when his desire to be with other men crossed some of our boundaries in communication and our relationships with others. I never lost that spark for him.

I'm worried he either has with me, or never had it once I came out.

❧

I WANT TO BE CLEAR; THIS IS NOT TO SAY THAT AIDEN has ever left me short of love, cuddles, partnership, equality in the household, or in terms of effort and contribution. He has been the perfect companionate partner, and he will be family no matter what transpires after the events that triggered this final chapter I'm writing.

I've asked so many people to be radically vulnerable in this compilation, so it would be unfair to expect them to do that without doing the same throughout this piece. It's harder to write this one than coming to terms with my sexual assaults, and I'm not being hyperbolic when I say that.

I do not love him any less, but I also do not think he finds me romantically or sexually attractive as a woman. The glowing on his face when he came home the other night, after which I'd find out he'd slept with a guy before we'd even had a chance to discuss our boundaries, let alone which ones shouldn't be crossed on this night that he totally wasn't going over there for that in the first place... He doesn't glow that way about me in that regard.

I suppose the argument could be made that we're married, and that kind of passion dies down after a while, but for me, it hasn't. But I also kind of saw it coming when he came out as gay, and even more so when he came out about his dynamic, which as it turns out, is the exact same as mine.

I had a very short relationship with another trans woman who had that, and after maybe once or twice in terms of intimacy, neither one of us sought it much because it wasn't what we wanted or needed.

It doesn't make either one of us bad people, but it does mean that it changes circumstances. That can't be denied here.

It's an odd place of serenity, really. I love this man so much that even if he doesn't find me sexually desirable, I want to support and encourage him to be who he is. I have seven more years on him, and I remember what it was like to be 25, to really begin to figure out who you are, not who your parents or high school friends told you that you were. I empathize because I've been warning him about this self-awareness since we've been together.

However, it's reasonable to say that for at least a good part of our time together, I wasn't expecting something like this to be a potential outcome.

It's also an odd place in that I have no real anger about the situation, even if it means he doesn't want to make love to me anymore, or even stay married to me. I've told him, and honestly at that, that I don't want or expect him to leave regardless of whether he wants to stay married to a woman who will have a vagina soon or not. I feel like we've been through too much together, and once again, we are amazing companionate partners, and for him, my love is infinite.

But I am not what or who he wants. Or needs. Or desires. Or lusts for.

I know, I know, you see the chapters where I admit that I'm gay as well, and it's true. But you know what? I was perfectly willing to be a lesbian married to a gay guy. On some level, you have to be a bit queer just to put up with me at all, I think. I radiate gayness, so it's all-encompassing in some sense. He's the only man I've ever been consensually involved with, and I've gone on one total date since coming out as trans with another guy, and felt nothing pretty much on the spot. Aiden was the exception, and still is.

That said, our intimacy always required a bit of lying in order to make it work. Either he had to pretend to be dominant, which he did for several lengthy stages in our marriage to this point, or we both had to pretend we were, shall we say, oppositely equipped.

But once our dynamic was the absolute same, and I will spare you the details or explanations on that front, it had to reset, naturally. Once you decide you can't be something for someone anymore, it has to change. There's no going back to the way it was. That once again doesn't make it a bad decision, or that it's anyone's fault; it's simply an acknowledgement of reality.

It's fair to say that Aiden didn't date nearly as much as I did for a while. Once he did start going out with guys, it was slightly difficult on me because cis men make me uncomfortable most of the time, and that seemed to be the basis of his attraction. We had very few boundaries, none of which I felt were unreasonable, but they seemed to get crossed. One time I didn't even find out until 35 days after the fact, and I was far more upset about that than what happened.

Let me see if I can explain this simply... I acknowledge that my husband is attracted to cis men. He is gay. He is not into women. Maybe he's into trans women, but I don't believe for a second he's interested in having sex with someone who has a vagina. That's inevitable at this point, as I wait for my three-month warning from the Mayo Clinic, knowing that I will be headed into the hospital and waking up as I always should have been.

I look at him, and the way he looks at me now, as opposed to before I started hormonally and socially transitioning, I don't feel like he lusts for me.

Now that he's 25, full of testosterone, and attracted to guys who are, well, guys... It's not a surprise to me that he went from talking to someone for the first time to sleeping with him in a week. That's like four weeks in gay. My jealousy comes not from the fact that he's sleeping with someone else, because we've had this arrangement since long before we were married, but from knowing that he doesn't want me like that.

I don't see him look at me the way he ogles Jason Momoa, and he's not glowing after spending time with me like he came home after the first night where he slept with this guy.

I can't be mad at him for doing what people who like each other and are in a relationship do, but I can feel hurt that I'm the one he married, yet he doesn't look at me like that.

He used to. When we were pretending to be cis and straight, he would glow like that. As transition took its toll on my, ahem, ability to perform in certain regards, he always said that it was okay. I hoped it would be, as soon it wouldn't even be an option.

But it reminded me of when an ex-fling found out about me well into transition. Her first reaction was, "Wow, that's such a waste!" in regard to my apparent primary function being a penis-haver who was sexually capable.

Now, I don't think he feels that I'm a waste, but he did marry me two months into my transition. He wasn't on hormones yet, and maybe that exacerbated the distance in our passion too, but he doesn't lust for me, and I've had to spend time coming to terms with that.

I just didn't expect it to happen so quickly.

Yes, I have two partners, and we have sex. I can only imagine that was difficult for him to come to terms with, but I also don't feel like I ever left him out of the equation, if that makes sense. I never felt like my changing sexuality precluded him.

And yes, this is something married couples deal with after they've been together for a while, but I've told him that he has to stop living in denial and lying to himself. He's spent so much time trying to be who he thinks he's supposed to be that he suppresses it and doesn't communicate with me.

I can't be mad at him for that. It takes a lot of energy to be with me. I am a high-maintenance pain in the ass, but I always felt like he was outsourcing the job to my other partners as a functioning unit, not as a handoff. I struggle between giving him the space to find out and explore who he really is, as a person and in his sexuality, and wanting him to be home with us, being a part of the family. Thankfully, Devyn isn't still in Seattle, or I'd be a wreck of emotions right now.

I'm needy. I get triggered easily. Being with me means you'll usually have to be the one to go to the store or pick up the medicine at the pharmacy. But I try to make up for it by writing beautiful love letters and poems, being there when you need it, and giving my all around the house and in the work I do. I'm high-maintenance, but I think I do my best to make it worth it.

His attention isn't here right now, and it wouldn't be whether he was going out every other day or not. I feel I owe him this space and chance to find out everything I had the chance to discover at age 25, because he got married so young and is with someone a touchdown ahead of him in age and experience.

But fuck, I miss him.

He's going on the third date in five days. Date four is the day after tomorrow. I'm letting him go because I want to give him that room and time, but also because his focus wouldn't be here if I refused.

If he's going to come to terms with how he feels, and figuring out if he still wants to be with me, it won't be because I kept him on a short leash and tried to repress who he is. I was with people who tried to repress my feminine thoughts and desires, and we all see how that worked out.

I never want to lose him, as a companion, partner, and family member. I love him so much, and I have shared a world of adventures with him in four years. I do not want them to end.

But I can't lie to myself, either, and neither can he. I know what he wants, and it isn't me, at least in that arena. That will either balance itself out after NRE subsides, or it won't, but living in denial won't change that result.

It'll be hard to not feel like I failed if he decides he doesn't want to be married to a vagina-having woman, since my first marriage was all sunshine and rainbows in its duration and quality alike, but I can't let that drive my decisions regarding the relationship, or my feelings regarding the reality of the situation.

I'm looking at the future of my life as it stands right

now, and knowing full well he will be involved somehow, but not being sure if that role will be as my husband or as a lover. I don't know if he will ever want me or look at me that way again, and that's where I find myself jealous of his new lover.

Not the time they're spending together or that they're sleeping together or that he seems to have more in common with him than he does me, but that when I got married again, I wanted my husband to want me like that, and I'm only now realizing that he did, for a time, but it was before I truly began to transition.

When it became every day and not just Monday nights. When the hormones affected my emotions and sexual function. When I was Marissa all the time and not just in certain company. When testosterone sent him into second puberty. When all of that happened, we still took care of each other, loved each other, worked hard, and contributed all we could to the betterment of the lives of our family. But the desire changed, and I don't know if it can ever be rekindled.

Is it wrong that I wish I was the one he wanted to fuck?

Is that verbose or TMI? He hasn't wanted to fuck me in a long time. We've made love, but we haven't... yeah. I never thought I'd be second fiddle in my own marriage, and that's no fault of either of ours. But just as he can't live in denial and pretend he feels a certain way about me, I can't live in denial and pretend I don't feel a certain way about it.

Fortunately there's an epilogue to this book, or this would be a fucking depressing entry to go out on. I don't know what will happen, as so much drastically altered the course of my life just from when I started putting together this project. I didn't know Emmalia that night at *The Vagina Monologues* at Penn, and here she is, featured more than any other writer not named Marissa McCool in this compilation.

Life changes, and it does so at a quicker rate than you're ever ready for, but pretending it doesn't is the worst decision you can make about that. Denial only makes the pain last longer and the uncertainty grow. The scar will cut deeper if it's drawn out.

I don't want it to be drawn out, regardless of what happens. I will always love him, no matter what, but I don't know if he'll ever want me again. I don't know how I feel about that, but I'm calmly serene talking about it, and I'll accept and support whatever he decides.

Though it's a shame that by next year's *Vagina Monologues*, if I'm invited, that I'll have a brand new, Mark Two (thanks, Bethany) science vagina, and the person to whom I'm married likely won't be the one who wants to fuck me. It is what it is, I suppose.

Fuck...

EPILOGUE

WHAT KIND OF DAY HAS IT BEEN?

by Marissa Alexa McCool

I DIDN'T SET OUT TO CHANGE THE WORLD WHEN I wrote my first book, *The PC Lie: How American Voters Decided I Don't Matter*, but I'd be a fool to say that my life didn't change nearly overnight with its publishing.

I'd been a miserable, vacant shell of a person, dying inside when the wrong name and pronouns were mentioned, doing a podcast that avoided specific issues so that I didn't bother anyone, and trying desperately to pretend to be whatever it is everyone wanted me to be.

When the election happened, all of that bitterness and rage came flying off the keyboard and into my book, and I could've left it there. I don't think anyone would've complained if I was the only one who wrote something in my own book, but that was never my style. I've always been the kind of person to acknowledge that many perspectives are different from mine, and I knew for sure the election results were affecting a great swath of populations and a lot of people were scared.

I specifically asked a few people who were prominent in various communities to write something. I also specifically asked the loves of my life to do the same. But even then, it wasn't enough. Was I willing to publish reactions from people I didn't know and had never met in order to create a greater spectrum of understanding the impact of that event?

Absolutely.

This is where *The Vagina Monologues* fell short for me, the people of color, and others who didn't feel their voices were represented in that show. What was a lot more real were the stories I heard in that circle.

When I was first coming out, it was just enough to be included in that kind of space. TERFs like to think that we somehow compromise women-only spaces by existing, and yet, if anyone were bothered by my presence in a women-only, super-feminist space, they sure didn't speak up about it. It's almost like I'm not a "separate" woman at all.

What I heard were stories. Real stories. From different voices, perspectives, and people.

I heard Meghana say how she didn't truly feel welcome.

I heard Sophia express amazing gratitude for the show itself, but go out of her way to make sure the intro specified differences that 90s feminism couldn't have possibly fore-seen being an issue, mostly because they weren't paying attention to voices that weren't their own.

I held Pearl in my arms for five solid minutes after the 2018 show, and no words were necessary, because we'd shared the important ones in a small black box theater many years ago, or in an otherwise-empty apartment.

I read the letter Sophia wrote for me to read in private after the show, and it still remains prominently on my Wall of Amazing. The same shelf where books signed by names like Margaret Atwood and Chris Kluwe rest. I hold the community I saw in that show on that level of regard.

Connor, Sophia, Pearl, Anonymous N, Meghana, Kellie... These, with Pearl being the exception, are names I know because of the Penn V-Day Community. Because Pearl wanted to put me in a show; not because I could act, although she knew I could, but because she wanted me to be *me*. In a place where others would affirm that. In a place where even if the words I was saying were pre-scripted, my walk and my voice really screamed: "I'm here, I'm alive, watch out!"

One year later, I was not only screaming things I wanted to say, but screaming for the chance for everyone on that stage to be afforded the same privilege I was given; being able to tell my own story. That's why I started writing this book.

I have stories about the people in this book, as they have their own stories. Some of them don't know who I am, because the prompt for this book brought me voices like Renee James, Jessica Kirschner, and Caren Evans. I knew I had to have my wonderful publisher, Amber, participate as she had in my first book. Accepting an essay from a stranger led to a wonderful friendship and business partnership.

I learned about Dharma Kelleher only a few months before I jokingly begged her to adopt me and be my trans mother on an interview on *The Inciting Incident Podcast* after hearing what a badass she was, and conversely, I offered to be a trans mom to three trans teens because I knew what it meant to have someone both affirm who you are and be able to call someone "Mom." Logan, Logan, and Lee are as dear to me as my own children, even though I've never met them in person. It doesn't matter. It never did.

My son, Michael, is being raised in a household with three parents, all of them transgender, and a sister, Kieran. He's already being brave by saying phrases like, "I don't have a dad," and pining to listen to voices like Noah Lugeons and Jenica Crail.

Kieran is a little activist who draws pictures for me and tells her class what it's like to have a trans mom. She's fearless.

Their other two parents are my husband, Aiden, and my partner, Devyn. If this is the first book you've ever read of mine, you may wonder why I have a poem about my girlfriend in here but not my husband or even my partner, and I encourage you to check out my previous books. My last book, *Passing Cars: The Internal Monologue of a Neurodivergent Trans Girl*, has an entire story about the unlikelihood of Aiden and I meeting, let alone getting married. The fact that we're still happily married despite both being gay is a testament to our love for one another.

Devyn often tells me, "You are my world." To go from a single, kinky life in Seattle to watching the kids after night shift and saving it up for the rare weekend getaway, that must mean something. I sit in their lap every morning before I go to work, and I love them no less than my husband.

I was all but ready to be sated with the only two non-women I'd ever dated living with me and that being that, and then Emmalia, my Priss, walked into my life and taught me to accept what I'd been running from my whole life.

I cannot for the life of me imagine what this would've been like if I was straight, monogamous, or religious. She's married, I'm married, and we're both gay. There were many ways that could've been impossible, but it wasn't.

Some people call me lucky for the school I went to or

the opportunities I've had because of my writing, podcasting, or activism. They're the biggest reason I feel lucky; I am not forced to limit my love, nor am I pressured by those I love to not love anyone else.

That circles back around to my original inspiration: Why should I be the only one allowed to tell my story?

I was able to address the lack of non-cis representation in the play through my words, and yet people like my husband felt entirely invisible because the pieces didn't even acknowledge him. I am a socially marginalized person, but I have never and will never have the experience of knowing how it feels to be targeted or silenced because of the color of my skin, despite what prominent talking heads think.

Melissa Frank may be a white queer person, but they used the stage of the March for our Lives to specify that all lives will not matter until black lives matter. They could've just talked about their son's life mattering, and instead they chose to speak up for so many parents and loved ones who felt a similar pain and were ignored by justice.

I will never know what cultural genocide truly means. A few years ago, it never dawned on me how offensive the Cleveland baseball mascot was, and then I listened to voices like Layha Spoonhunter. By then, I'd already heard the native voices in Flint and regretted that tattoo more than most anything in my life, but I'd not only been brought up in a society that didn't consider those voices, but did all it could to erase them from existence entirely.

Brave Crow's words may be harsh to those who aren't aware of just how heartbreaking it is to have culture lost and buried under blood and broken promises, but they say their words loud because they need to be said.

Meghana had to fight to have the line "my saree is not

an excuse to fetishize me" included in her performance of the piece "My Short Skirt." All I had to do was show up and not even memorize my lines that I'd written and would scream into a microphone simply because I asked if I could be in the show as an alum.

That was not acceptable. I asked Meghana to write the foreword of this book because they can teach me much more about being in this society, and certain exclusive groups, as a person with brown skin and a non-white-sounding name, same as I can teach her much about walking into a room and hoping that the first question someone asks me isn't about what's in my underwear.

When I read the words of Melissa and Anonymous K, their words haunted me with visual imagery for days, the same as when I heard Meghana tell the truth about how she felt to be minimized in the show, similarly but distinctly different from how I had as the only trans person there.

I saw how those with brown and black skin tensed up as someone talked about the whimsy and fun of 90s feminism by a girl who I'm sure was well-intended, but that's the point. Just being well-intended and not aware isn't enough anymore. People of color and trans people are assaulted and murdered, and the perpetrators get off with panic defenses and Blue Lives Mattering. It may seem harmless in a circle of 70 people, but existing while having dark skin or being trans in and of itself is dangerous.

And while a show that focuses mostly on the issues of white, cis feminism may be very entertaining and necessary to get some feet in the door of feminism, it's not enough when others are saying, "We feel left out. These are not our experiences."

Callie Wright and Mandisa Thomas, two of the best activists I know and people I'm proud to consider friends, showed me the way to speak up for those communities: listen.

Brave Crow taught me the best way to use my Two-Spirit T-shirt, as I'd been socially adopted into the Two-Spirit movement and could therefore support an indigenous artist and bring awareness with my platform: listen.

Meghana showed me that I had a lot to learn about being an activist, and that there were many voices I needed to not speak for, but to listen to. She's the reason this book exists. She's the reason I compiled as many voices as I could, some of whom I haven't even mentioned here, but do know that I love and value all their contributions. I listened to all of them, even the ones I didn't know.

You don't have to know someone to listen to their experience or trust their perspective. That's what intersectionality truly is, and until white men stop playing the Identity Politics card when something other than their issues, or them being treated as the universal default, is acknowledged, we will constantly be fighting the battle of slurs, snowflakes, and safe space clichés that will always be thrown down by those who support the status quo and have no interest or awareness about changing that. The unspoken.

Previously, anyway.

ACKNOWLEDGMENTS

Aiden, Devyn, and Priss. Nathanial, Michael, and Kieran. Logan, Logan, and Dee.

My family, blood and chosen.

Eve Ensler.

Every writer who participated, by name or anonymously.

Rachael Gunderson.

Dara Hoffman-Fox.

Karen Garst.

Amber Biesecker-Singletary.

Wyrmwood Publishing.

Callie Wright.

NaNoCon 2018.

The University of Pennsylvania V-Day community.

The Daily Pennsylvanian.

Erin Cross.

Pearl Lo.

Sophia Griffith-Gorgati.

Glenda Jordan.

Dr. Rosemary Malague.

Dharma Kelleher.

University of Minnesota-Duluth English postgrad.

All listeners, especially Patreon donors, of my podcasts.

Everyone who pre-ordered this book, which was the most since *The PC Lie* in 2016.

ABOUT THE AUTHOR

Marissa, 32, is a wife, partner, parent, podcaster, activist, speaker, and now an author of five books. She graduated the University of Pennsylvania cum laude in 2017 with degrees in English, Cinema and Media Studies, and Anthropology. She has been published by *The Huffington Post, Psychology Today, Lords of Pain, Intentional Insights, Faithless Feminist, Snarky Feminist,* and her own blog, *Marissa Explains it All,* not to mention countless guest spots on podcasts in addition to her own shows.

For more information:
rismccool.com
rismcwriting@gmail.com

CPSIA information can be obtained
at www.ICGtesting.com
Printed in the USA
BVHW070330151218
535692BV00012B/207/P